D1567280

Challenging
Units  for Gifted Learners

Challenging Units for Gifted Learners

TEACHING THE WAY GIFTED STUDENTS THINK

Kenneth J. Smith, Ph.D.

PRUFROCK PRESS INC.
WACO, TEXAS

Copyright © 2010, Prufrock Press Inc.
Edited by Jennifer Robins
Cover and Layout Design by Marjorie Parker

ISBN-13: 978-1-59363-421-6

No part of this book may be reproduced, translated, stored in a retrieval system, or transmitted, in any form or by any means, electronic, mechanical, photocopying, microfilming, recording, or otherwise, without written permission from the publisher.

Printed in the United States of America.

At the time of this book's publication, all facts and figures cited are the most current available. All telephone numbers, addresses, and website URLs are accurate and active. All publications, organizations, websites, and other resources exist as described in the book, and all have been verified. The author and Prufrock Press Inc. make no warranty or guarantee concerning the information and materials given out by organizations or content found at websites, and we are not responsible for any changes that occur after this book's publication. If you find an error, please contact Prufrock Press Inc.

Prufrock Press Inc.
P.O. Box 8813
Waco, TX 76714-8813
Phone: (800) 998-2208
Fax: (800) 240-0333
http://www.prufrock.com

Being gifted "must be understood as a qualitatively distinct characteristic. It is not a matter of degree but of a different quality of experiencing: vivid, absorbing, penetrating, encompassing, complex, commanding—a way of being quiveringly alive."

—Michael Piechowski (1992, p. 181)

Dedication

This book is dedicated to three great teachers: first, to Joanna Williams, my advisor at Columbia University, for changing the way I think and for inspiring this book; second, to Richard Dolezal, my department chair at the Latin School of Chicago, for teaching me the joy of scholarship; and third, to Jerry White, my first camp director, for showing me that there are different ways to be smart.

Contents

Acknowledgements

Many people played an important role in the creation of this book. I'd like to thank the teachers who gave me feedback and inspiration or who piloted aspects of the units: JoAnn Tennenbaum, Sunset Ridge School District 29 in Northfield, IL; Cheri Brill, Community Consolidated School District in Buffalo Grove, IL; Josie Sherrer, formerly of the University of Miami, Miami, FL; and Marcia Hickey from Children's Engineering Educators in Richmond, VA. It was their input that helped me better understand what teachers needed to hear and how best to say it. Each in her own way showed me that a smart teacher is worth her weight in gold. I would also like to thank Roger Hickey for continual proof-reading of draft after draft and Jennifer Farr for her work on the bibliography and her help with the research. Without their help, my deficiencies would still be evident in my writing.

It would have been impossible for me to write this had it not been for all of my former students with their traditional and nontraditional intellectual gifts. So many of them remain vivid in my mind, from the extortionist in my very first classroom to the third grader who just recently was in a class where I was explaining how a small suburb and big city could both be called communities. She slowly raised her hand and, when called on, said, "The Earth is sort of a big community." When I asked her how so, she added, "Well, we are all sort of in this life together." They all showed me that a brilliant mind in a student is forever a fascinating thing to observe, a huge responsibility to teach, and a continuous source of inspiration. I thank all of those students across the years for helping me understand that.

Finally I would like to thank (is there a stronger, more heartfelt word for my appreciation here?) Jennifer Robins, my editor, who saw this project through from proposal to publication. As solitary as writing was, it was Jennifer's ability to balance her respect for an author's words with guidance on how to make content and structure clearer that got me through the process. If this book proves worth reading, it is due to her help.

Chapter 1

Introduction: We Are Intellectual Archeologists

The creation of a thousand forests is in one acorn.

—Ralph Waldo Emerson

Three True Stories

A teacher with whom I enjoy working once complained to me that one of her students should not receive gifted services because he was lazy. "He never finishes his math boxes so why provide enrichment activities for him?" Later that day, I asked him why he hadn't finished his math boxes, the morning math challenges. He told me that he had gotten distracted by trying to calculate mentally the number of cement blocks in one of the classroom walls. Without counting each block, but by extrapolating from the pattern of the first two rows, he had gotten the number right. I had known since he was in second grade that he was much brighter than I am—probably brighter than anyone else in the building.

While I was in New York working on my dissertation, I stopped in one of those ubiquitous Chinese fast food restaurants that lined the lower West side. Ahead of me in line were three very young, very pregnant girls. From their conversation, I guessed that they were taking a summer class for unwed mothers and each had been given a budget by the program with which to buy lunch. Two of the girls were immobile in line trying to figure out from the wall menu what to order and how to divvy up the costs. The third girl rattled off several suggestions that would be divided unevenly as would the costs. She then figured each girl's contribution and change instantly in her head. I have often wondered if anyone, including her, had valued her rapid-fire math skills.

Not too long ago, I was working with a junior high language arts class on adding mood-evoking pictures to poetry podcasts. I stopped to read the poem of one girl; it was stunning in its imagery and subtle complexity, reminiscent of Emily Dickinson. I had known the student for years and thought that she was a better-than-average writer. However, because I had never engaged her in a poetry project, I had completely missed her true gift.

The point of starting with these stories is that, although there are many children with exceptional gifts who test well, appear precocious before starting school, and earn good grades, there are also extraordinary youngsters in our classrooms whose gifts are not as easily recognized. We therefore need to strive to understand and respond to the giftedness in our students by continually digging until we uncover each child's strengths. We must be intellectual archeologists. I hope that this book gives teachers additional tools with which to uncover these gifts.

Three factors underlie the projects presented in the following chapters: (a) the unique way gifted students think; (b) the role of content-specific, expert knowledge; and (c) the role of the teacher/mentor in instructing gifted learners. Each of these influences is discussed below.

Qualitatively Different Thinking of Gifted Learners

This book is written from a cognitive psychology perspective. I begin by reviewing current research that offers insight into the distinctions between the thinking of gifted and more typical students. In compiling the research for this discussion, my focus has been on explaining—not just listing—the intellectual processes in which gifted students engage, particularly those that they use in structuring and solving open-ended problems. I detail how these processes operate and how they are observed. Following this review of the research, the remainder of this book offers units that both challenge and develop those cognitive processes.

Hertberg-Davis and Callahan (2008) reported that gifted students often have to wait until Advanced Placement (AP) courses in their final high school years to enjoy the academic challenges that they had found lacking throughout their educational careers. However, research indicates that appropriately serving advanced learners requires an infusion of higher level challenges into the sequences of classes that they encounter throughout all of their school years—beginning in the early grades. Therefore, this book is designed to help you present units that gifted learners will find challenging and that will foster their complex thinking— beginning in the early grades. It is written to appeal to students with a range of intellectual gifts and learning styles, and to help you keep them engaged across grades and content areas.

Domain-Specific Knowledge

Each book in the Challenging Units for Gifted Learners series presents various units based on in-depth, domain-specific knowledge of central principles and content. To develop mastery of this complex, domain-specific knowledge, Bass, Magone, and Glaser (2002) recommended that students demonstrate an understanding of both the principles and the complex problem-solving procedures that are particular to the content area at hand. This is because it is an understanding of domain-specific principles and problem-solving procedures that separates beginners from experts in particular subject areas. In physics, for example, the domain-specific principle may be a law of inertia. For fiction writers, the principle may be that juxtaposing images creates complexity in a character. In each of these examples, principles or cause-and-effect relationships are domain-specific; nevertheless, in both domains, it is a grasp of principle-based, procedural knowledge that characterizes the experts. Thus, in writing each book in the series, I begin by asking what are the core principles and concepts of the domain at hand.

The books also require that students explore this domain-specific knowledge in depth. The National Research Council suggests that in-depth learning occurs not from memorizing material from a text or lecture, but from successfully transferring core, principle-based knowledge from one situation to another (Bransford, Brown, & Cocking, 1999). Yet, it is this former knowledge base that so many equate with high-level understanding. According to Moon (2008), if a teacher believes that knowing facts is what is important rather than big ideas and conceptual understanding, then how could the gifted student be challenged? For example, on a recent episode of *Jeopardy*, one of the categories was 20th Century American Poets. As the questions became more arcane, the prize money jumped. But is this factual recall reflective of gifted-level insight in the language arts?

According to Anderson (2005), regardless of the subject area, more successful learners tend to see knowledge as overlapping networks of facts, often related by cause and effect or other procedural insight. For example, the knowledge needed to appreciate Emily Dickinson might center around how her compressed and, at times, inverted sentence structure supported her multifaceted use of a single image. This then raises the questions, "What does it mean to have expertise in poetry?" and "How should an understanding of this expertise drive instruction for both gifted students and their more typical counterparts?"

For me, the answer to these ongoing questions is that we need to gear instruction for all students to these big ideas and conceptual, principled knowledge and guide students to use these principles to drive their academic problem solving. To do this well, we first need to understand how successful learners are thinking when they are solving complex problems and then provide instruction that both challenges and nurtures this kind of thinking in our students.

The Teacher's Role in Fostering Intellectual Gifts

Research suggests that people who reach expert levels of understanding might be highly gifted in the first place, but that they still need training and practice to develop their gifts. There are several specific accounts of genius that show the need for teachers and mentors to guide their development and to maximize their potential.

Being in this role is a huge responsibility. Just think about little Albert Einstein doing poorly in his elementary grades. It was not until his uncle began teaching him number tricks that he became excited about math. What would have happened if his uncle hadn't intervened when teachers had failed? I wonder what happened to all of the other little Alberts who had the talent but not the teacher? That is part of what motivates us to teach—at least it is for me. Thus, we see that, as teachers, we have a particular obligation to recognize the potential for greatness in our students and to nurture their gifts as they reach expertise—and beyond.

In Bloom's (1985) work on creative children, he pointed out that although gifted musicians started training early, they also showed a proclivity for their eventual expertise before this training began. The musicians were described as quick to learn the piano and were recognized as gifted by their parents before beginning lessons. What seems equally relevant to the recognition of talent in Bloom's work is the role of the teacher. "[The prodigies] training began in early childhood with warm and loving teachers who were then supplanted by more demanding and rigorous master teachers" (Winner, 2000, p. 160).

Finally, in considering the teacher's role in carrying out the projects presented here, I am reminded of Scarr's (1997; see Feldhusen 2005) point that nature does not give gifts; it gives genetic potential. In comparison to their age-level peers, some children are fortunate enough to be born with the potential to learn material earlier and faster, to handle more complexity and abstraction, and to solve complex problems better. This potential, however, needs stimulating experiences from home and school or it will not unfold (Feldhusen, 2005). This book is designed to help teachers provide the stimulating curricula that will nurture this potential. The projects presented here are based on research into how these students actually think differently from their peers and how they use their learning styles and potentials not merely to develop intellectual expertise, but to move beyond expertise to the production of new ideas. I am hopeful that through these units, students will develop their superior abilities because we have understood and encouraged their unique way of thinking.

I believe that the core of being intellectually gifted is thinking that is qualitatively different from the way most people think. Giftedness is about processing in a more complex way. The subsequent chapters in this book present units that foster and develop this kind of thinking.

Chapter 2

What Are They Thinking? The Cognitive Processes of Gifted Learners

I like a teacher who gives you something to take home to think about besides homework.

—Edith Ann (Lily Tomlin)

In this chapter, I discuss the ways that gifted learners think. This discussion will extend statements of what these students *do* intellectually, to explain *how* they think when facing intellectual challenges. For example, one well-composed list of what gifted learners do included statements such as: they "readily grasp underlying principles and can often make valid generalizations about events, people, or objects" and they "process materials at a much greater depth" (Rhode Island Gifted Association, n.d., para. 3, 6). Rather than simply name these behaviors, I explain the cognition in which gifted learners engage that allows them to grasp the underlying principles or to process at a greater depth.

After this discussion of the research, the subsequent chapters each present a unit for gifted instruction with which you can support and develop these cognitive processes in your gifted students. This chapter presents the theoretical justification for the rest of the book. Each unit is readily adaptable to a variety of small-group and whole-class needs. Moreover, they can be adapted to different junior high grade levels. The Freudian analysis of literature unit, for example, is written for a small group within a heterogeneously grouped class. Suggestions are offered, however, for teaching it to a whole class and for changing the book being analyzed from *Lord of the Flies* to others that may be better suited to the grade level with which you are dealing.

The Research

Compared to the research in other areas of cognitive psychology, the research on gifted learners appears to be particularly incomplete. This is due, in part, to the fact that research tends to follow state mandates that are usually funded, and those rarely include gifted education. Besides specific research on gifted learners, however, concomitant areas of psychological research provide insight into how our students think, and I draw on these bodies of research to present a more complete picture of the gifted student. First, I look at the brain scan research. The recent growth of this research (e.g., Eide & Eide, 2004)—studies that record brain activity during cognitive tasks—is providing insight into how gifted brains actually function. This is beginning to fill in some of the gaps in the research on gifted learners.

Second, there is a large body of cognitive research in expertise and problem solving that has implications for gifted instruction. This is particularly relevant because several—but not all—current definitions of giftedness include problem-solving ability (e.g., Sternberg's and Gardner's definitions, as discussed later in this chapter). Although the fields of gifted education and cognitive psychology both include studies related to giftedness, the two areas have traditionally stood apart (Hettinger & Carr, 2003, as discussed in Dixon, 2008.) By drawing from all of these research areas, I hope to provide a more complete picture of how gifted children think than I could by presenting either area in isolation.

It has been my experience that there is a great deal to be learned about gifted students from the research on expert problem solvers. This must be done cautiously, however, as "expert" and "gifted" are not synonymous. One of the most important differences between the two terms is the belief of some researchers (e.g., Gagné, 1995) that "gifted" is seen as having a significant genetic component, while other researchers (e.g., Ericsson, Krampe, & Tesch-Römer, 1993) believe that with the right experiences, most of us can develop expertise in a particular field. Finally, there is evidence suggesting that people with extremely high IQs do not simply emulate experts but have problem-solving skills unique to their ability group (e.g., Smith, 2004). Still, if we accept these caveats, examining the relationship between experts and gifted thinkers provides a unique insight into gifted students' cognition.

So, Who Are These Gifted Students?

Precisely defining "gifted thinking" is an onerous task. Traditionally, gifted students have been defined as intellectually advanced. And, intellectually advanced has been defined as scoring in the top few percentiles on standardized IQ assessments or formal tests of school-based knowledge. Hoh (2008) called this method of defining "gifted" as problematic because these tests "will correlate directly with intellectual ability if this is how the gifted have been identified in the first place" (p. 58). That is, the test identifies people who do what the test asks, but that doesn't mean that the test uses the correct definition of gifted thinking.

In discussing the limitation of definitions based solely on test scores, Sousa (2003) noted that visual-spatial reasoning may be as important as verbal skills in defining intelligence. The latter, however, is clearly more central in both standardized achievement tests and group-administered IQ tests. This predominate focus on verbal intelligence at the expense of other qualities highlights the need to expand traditional test-based definitions of IQ to include students with other talents, such as the ability to solve complex visual-spatial problems. Or perhaps, as discussed below, creativity—the ability to develop new insight or products from existing knowledge—is an integral ingredient in identifying giftedness for some students. For other students, complex analytical thinking may be the defining characteristic of their gifts. For the purposes of this book, gifted thinking is defined as superior in its complexity, and this complexity is explicated in the remainder of this chapter.

From my experiences, students who do well on IQ tests are intellectually exceptional. Children can't fake a high-IQ score or achieve it by chance. However, the converse is most definitely not true. Doing poorly on the test does not necessarily mean that a student has a lower IQ than those whose score high on an intelligence test. It might just as well mean that the test and the taker were out of sync. A student who scores poorly may be an unmotivated test taker or gifted in nontraditional ways. Precocious children in the younger grades may get fatigued and give up or run out of time. In short, it is a lot easier to identify who is gifted than it is to identify who isn't.

When it comes to defining gifted students, equally important to test success should be a child's ability to engage in complex, rarefied thinking. Moreover, identifying this complex thought becomes a precursor to understanding not simply who gifted learners are, but what they are doing intellectually that distinguishes them. These intellectual strengths cut across content areas (verbally gifted or mathematically gifted), across models (e.g., Gardner, 1983, 1993; Sternberg, 1997), problem types (well-defined or ill-defined), and thinking styles (analytical or creative).

In the rest of this chapter, I detail what the research says distinguishes gifted thinking from the more typical so that teachers can identify this complex thought process. I then connect this research into a unified model of how gifted learners use their intellectual strengths to solve problems and meet intellectual challenges. In the final section of this chapter, I present an overview of how this understanding of gifted students' cognition structures provides the rationale for the units presented in this book.

PRECOCIOUSNESS

Often, children will reveal cognitive or artistic abilities that significantly exceed those possessed by other members of their age group. They may, for example, walk, read, or play piano earlier than one would normally expect. Children who exhibit this kind of advanced intellectual development may be considered gifted (Hoh, 2008; Koshy & Robinson, 2006). Because precocious youngsters hold the promise of great achievement, we have a particular responsibility to their education.

Early reading is one of the most powerful indicators of exceptional giftedness. Both Terman (Terman & Lima, 1926) and Hollingworth (1926, 1942) reported that early reading most clearly differentiated between the moderately and highly gifted children in their studies. This precociousness often indicates that those children who exhibit early glimmers of exceptional intellect will not only continue to grasp concepts faster than their more typical peers, but will do so with less practice.

Precociousness may extend beyond a particular content area; it may evidence itself as general intellectual prowess. In these cases, young children may, across subject areas, think differently from their peers. Sternberg and Lubart (1992) and Hoh (2008), for example, pointed out that precocious children are particularly aware of critically relevant information—that is, information that is salient to the information at hand—whereas their peers often fail to distinguish the significant from the less relevant. "Supposedly, the gifted are more perceptually sensitive" (Hoh, 2008, p. 60). This perceptual acuity seems to cross domains in indicating talented students.

High achievement by young, nongifted children can prove unstable (Robinson, 2008). Early accomplishments in domains such as math or reading, however, tend to correlate with high achievement later in school (Hollingworth, 1926, 1942; Terman & Lima, 1926). When it comes to curriculum for these students, we obviously can't wait and see if these youngsters will blossom into official "geniuses" before adapting their curriculum; we need to provide for our gifted students at all grades. All students need programs in which they can achieve their potential—even very bright children. Not recognizing precociousness can prove devastating to young gifted learners. As Gross (1999) noted, highly gifted children are frequently placed at risk in the early years of school through missed identification, inappropriate grade placements, and inadequate curriculum.

For much of the last century, many psychologists argued that a child's inborn IQ was the source of prodigious talent. More recently, some scholars have proposed that IQ is insignificant when compared to the right practice and dedication (see Feldman, 2008, for a review). For the purposes of this book, I have taken an interactive view—as have many psychologists (e.g., Feldman & Katzir, 1998). That is, children are born with a potential for intellectual accomplishments, but teachers are a great force for providing (or limiting) this potential. Moreover, I further believe that few of us reach the absolute maximum of our potential and that with the right guidance children can always move further.

In this section, I have noted that being precocious is more complicated than simply learning earlier than other students do. It also means thinking about and remembering content in a more complex way. To best match curriculum to the needs of these special learners, we need to understand the uniqueness of how they retain information. Explaining this is the goal of the following section.

MEMORY AND THE ORGANIZATION OF KNOWLEDGE

Memory, perhaps more than any other aspect of intelligence, significantly characterizes a person's cognitive abilities. To anyone who has worked with gifted students, it is evident that they are able to retain more information with less practice than typical students. Moreover, studies support that gifted children have superior memories in their areas of strength (Winner, 1996). Students with language gifts, for example, are better able to recall linguistic information than numerical and spatial information, whereas mathematically gifted students, in contrast, showed the opposite pattern (Dark & Benbow, 1991; see Hoh, 2008, for a review).

Research also shows that gifted learners are better able to retain information with less iteration. Therefore, they do not need the same amount of review that others do. Julian Stanley, who founded the Study of Mathematically Precocious Youth (SMPY) at Johns Hopkins University, often pointed out that repeated review is more than a waste of time for students gifted in math and science. Students are significantly more likely to forget or mislearn content in these areas when they must drill and review it more than two or three times (Rogers, 2002).

Gifted learners also are hypersensitive to information at an early age (Hoh, 2008). Their first impressions are more vivid than most, and they are aware of more details in their surroundings. Therefore, they take in more as they register new information and details others tend to miss. Brain scan research suggests that forming these kinds of rich initial impressions characterize brain activity in gifted learners. Functional magnetic resonance imaging (FMRI) of gifted thinkers as memories are first registering show that their brain activity is especially intense and enduring. Moreover, these scans are also frequently characterized as multimodal, involving activity in brain areas that store many different types of memories, such as personal associations; different sensory modalities like color, sound, smell, or visual images; or verbal or factual impressions. This multimodality means that gifted thinkers often make connections in ways other people don't. They frequently have special abilities in associational thinking such as analogy and metaphor and in analytical or organizational skills through which diverse associations are understood and systematized (Eide & Eide, 2004)

Although there are multiple paradigms for describing the organization of memory, many cognitive theorists appear to agree that human memory can be conceived of as two stores: working memory and long-term memory (see Anderson, 2005, for a review). Working memory refers to memory that is currently active, whereas long-term memory refers to well-learned memories that are stored in the brain, but are not currently being thought about. Whether or not we ever forget things that have been stored in long-term memory or simply cannot retrieve them is still being debated in the literature and has been since the 1950s.

A series of recent experiments have indicated in which sections of the brain cognitive activity related to memory storage actually takes place. In one study, Gabrieli (2001) found that the left frontal lobe is more active during the processing of verbal material while the right frontal lobe is more active in the processing of visual imagery.

In recent years, the use of FMRIs (Eide & Eide, 2004) shows qualitative differences between the memory-related brain activity of gifted and more typical thinkers. This brain activity not only suggests that the initial impressions are especially detailed in gifted thinkers, but also that activity during later recollections is often unusually intense or vivid. "Because vivid initial impressions correlate with better recollection, gifted brains are also characterized by increased memory efficiency and capacity" (Eide & Eide, 2004, para. 2). These findings that explain brain structure and functioning provide insight into why gifted students can register and recall domain-specific information better that most of us do. More important, they support the development of gifted curriculum that is content-rich beyond what is expected of more typical learners. This is because their brains seem ready to address complexity before many of their ages would suggest.

For gifted learners, the important memory issue extends beyond how much information they can hold in working memory and how long they can maintain it. In developing curriculum for these students, we also need to understand the unique ways in which information is organized in their long-term memory. In understanding this, we can develop curriculum that facilitates both their superior organization of knowledge and its retrieval.

An early and often-cited study in the problem-solving research addresses this concern. In this study, expert and novice chess players tried to recreate groups of chess positions on a game board (Chase & Simon, 1973). The experts were much better at recalling the positions when the pieces were arranged in meaningful, real-game arrangements. However, when the pieces were arranged in arbitrary nongame groupings, their recall matched that of nonexperts. This seminal study suggests that being able to establish meaningful connections that chunk related information together in memory may facilitate recall by talented learners. Thus, although we all recall basically the same number of chunks, experts' chunks of information are more elaborate and complex than that of more typical learners.

A more recent study compared the memory of gifted and typical math students. The mathematically gifted students proved superior not only in the amount of information stored, but also in the kind of information stored, such as mathematical patterns and problem-solving methodologies (Hermelin & O'Connor, 1990). These students had a keen recall of an arsenal of math-specific strategies for efficient solving of challenging problems.

These experiments suggest that gifted students tend to store facts around intricate networks related to meaningful concepts. More typical learners, in contrast, have fewer elaborated connections among the information stored in long-term memory, and fewer elaborations make retrieval more difficult. Quillian (1966) called these elaborated concepts *semantic networks* and described them as web-like structures that represent connections (i.e., nodes) among pieces of information in memory. They can represent both conceptual and concrete knowledge. A child's semantic network of dinosaurs, for example, might have central nodes naming the dinosaurs. These central nodes might then be associated to each other through such links as "is a," "has a," and "eats" (Chi & Koeske, 1983). Properties that are common characteristics between two dinosaurs link them together. Two dinosaurs might be linked together because they are meat eaters, but would not have a common "lived during" link if one had lived during the Jurassic period and the other during the Triassic period. Thus, with a sophisticated understanding of how details are related, a student's semantic network can become quite elaborate and hierarchical. More complicated networks, in turn, facilitate students' recall of information. "Extra and better structured knowledge has been a pervasive concept generally used for interpreting better memory performance" (Chi & Koeske, 1983).

According to Anderson (2005), the strength of the connections between facts and concepts is determined by frequency of experience. What Anderson does not address, however, is that as IQ increases, the number of times a person needs to hear or experience a fact decreases (Gross, 1995). This fact will be central to the instruction offered in this book. If a child with an IQ of 145 needs to hear a fact one time to internalize it and a child with a similar learning style but with an IQ of 100 needs to hear it three times, then the brighter child is spending too much time waiting for the other child to catch up. Therefore, each chapter in this book presents unique options for instructing the gifted children in your classroom so that they are not waiting while other children strive to understand a concept they have already grasped.

A theoretical alternative explanation for how we organize information in memory is called *schema* (often pluralized as schemata). This concept grew out of early work in artificial intelligence, although Piaget used the term in developmental psychology literature in 1926. A schema is an abstracted mental structure that represents a person's understanding of some aspect of the world (e.g., a restaurant or a short story). A schema has slots for actual features and values that members of the category possess. These slots are filled in with specific details of the exemplar at hand. For example, a partial schema for a mystery might be represented as:

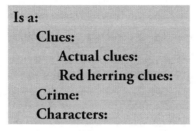

In this schema, *Actual clues* is a slot, and items such as *broken window, brick inside house*, and *footprints* could be specific features for the story at hand that could be used to substantiate that slot. A great deal of research has focused on story schemas or story structures (e.g., Gardill & Jitendra, 1999; Stein & Glenn, 1977) and their impact on instruction, although much of it seems to focus on students with learning disabilities and typical students.

Through the instantiation of schema, students have to put little energy into understanding newly encountered exemplars. The more slots that someone's schema has, the more elaborate and facile the understanding, assuming, of course, that the categories are correct. In the units presented in this book, I assume that students need less time to add elaborations to existing schemas and are comfortable with more details because their semantic networks and schemata are more sophisticated.

NEW INFORMATION

In their areas of strength, gifted learners are taking in and processing more external input than do more typical people. This increased input needs to be organized so as not to be overwhelming. To accomplish this, people with talent in a particular area may be relating this input to networks and schemas already established in long-term memory.

In the early problem-solving research (e.g., Shepard & Teghtsoonian, 1961), psychologists thought that approximately seven (plus or minus two) tidbits of information could be held in working memory. More could be held if these tidbits could be linked together in meaningful ways. With the current brain research, however, it appears that the prefrontal areas have a variety of storage centers for taking in and processing different kinds of information (Anderson, 2005). With this current body of research, it seems that most people are aware of much more information than the big seven plus or minus two, but forget it rapidly. Gifted people, in contrast, seem to have a better ability to retain this information and to connect it to information already retained in the internal hypothalamus regions—to engage more of the brain in the creation of memories (Eide & Eide, 2004; Gross, 1995). This qualitatively different brain activity is what Eide and Eide (2004) refer to as "brains on fire" because FMRI brain scans of gifted people reveal so much extra activity that they look like photographs of fires. Brain scans of more typical people who are exposed to the same stimuli show much less activity, and the color patterns revealed in the scan therefore seem much calmer.

By exploring the nature of precocious thinking and the structure and efficiency of gifted students' memory, we begin to form a picture of gifted students' thinking processes. This, in turn, suggests the following guidelines for developing curriculum that will foster this kind of reasoning, although we need to be cautious of overinterpreting research findings.

1. Gifted students seem to be able to handle large amounts of content, even at a young age. This means more than declarative information, such as principle-based concepts that relate these facts through cause and effect or logical patterns.

2. Gifted students take in information more rapidly than most students in their age group, often waiting for these other students to learn through repeated experiences what they learn with little iteration. Therefore, they can be given or encouraged to discover larger amounts of information.

3. As students process this new information, much of it is connected to existing concept structures' already stored in memory. Relating this new information to these existing structures allows gifted thinkers to make connections, elaborations, and manipulations that might escape more typical students in their age group.

INSTANCE THEORY

Earlier, I discussed schemas and semantic networks as ways in which students integrate new knowledge into existing knowledge. Teachers should be aware, however, that some cognitive psychologists have explored an alternative explanation of how information is organized and stored in memory: instance theory (e.g., Anderson, 2005).

Both schemas and semantic networks are abstracted from repeated experiences. Instance theory is quite different from either of these. According to instance theory, rather than holding a schema or a semantic network in long-term memory, people maintain knowledge of a specific representative example in long-term memory. They then judge new instances against this prototypical model to decide what it is (Anderson, 2005). For instance, a child seeing an emu for the first time might have difficulty deciding if it is a bird because it is only similar to a robin—the prototype of a bird—in some ways. Thus, the more different an example is from the prototype, the more difficult it is to comprehend. Although a literature review found no specific study of how gifted students use these prototypes, I find that my students' representative examples have a great deal more detail and thus can see connections with distally related examples that others might miss. This may shed some light on why they seem more comfortable with complexity and why they seem to easily make connections between two seemingly disparate topics—they see relationships to details in their prototypes that others do not have. Although much research has been conducted into which type of theory is correct, recent research tends to focus on when people use each model.

Principled Knowledge or What Does It Mean to Know Something Well?

In comparison to their age peers, gifted learners not only take in more external stimuli, they also use more areas of their brains in processing this information (Eide & Eide, 2004). Moreover, evidence suggests that they perceive this extensive input as being "organized information" (Hoh, 2005). To do this, they abstract essential features and see them as connected. Research in several content areas provides evidence that this superior ability to abstract and generalize is a significant part of what defines gifted performance. For example, as discussed in Hoh (2005), Krutetskii (1976) found that high-ability sixth- and seventh-grade mathematicians reported a déjà vu experience when encountering new problems. They felt as if they had previously encountered problems of similar structure but with different values. This seems quite similar to developing problem-solving schema based on previously encountered examples of similar problems. These are based on mathematical principles needed to solve a class of problems. Gifted students then substantiate these schemas with the values in each new problem.

Chi, Feltovich, and Glaser (1981) drew similar conclusions that principle-based knowledge characterizes experts. They asked expert and novice physicists to sort physics experiments by type. The novices tended to sort by concrete surfaces, such as "contains blocks on an incline plane." The experts, in contrast, identified similarity through the physics principles used to solve the problems: "These can be solved by Newton's second law." Clearly, the path to success in solving these problems lies in seeing similar patterns to solution principles, not in the objects being mentioned in the problems. More recently, Shavinina and Kholodnaja (1996) observed that high school students who were gifted in math organized their knowledge around general categories while their more average subjects' categories were based on specific items in the problems. Similarly, Winner (1996) found that a 7-year-old musical prodigy saw patterns in music and used these patterns to improvise new music that fit into the background because he could easily hear the overriding structure of the style.

It appears that across domains, gifted students are able to abstract generalizable principles and procedures from specific examples. In turn, this facilitates students' solving of new problems even when the objects in the problem appear quite different from previous examples. Therefore, gifted students not only handle more information quickly, they also abstract key features from this information so that future problem solving of the same kind occurs with fewer processing demands than did the early examples.

Studies of expert/novice differences suggest that the course of knowledge acquisition proceeds from a declarative (sometimes called propositional) form to a principle-based, procedural form (Anderson, 2005; Glaser, 1989; Williams, 2002). This procedural knowledge is much more predictive of problem-solving success (Anderson, 2005). For example, the physicists in the Chi et al. (1981) experiment who saw the simple machine type as the central feature would find fewer problem-solving strategies in the problem than would the experts who saw physics principles as the central feature. Likewise, Williams (2002) studied expert and novice athletes and found that the experts were more likely to focus on subtle cues that indicated their opponent's next procedure and anticipate response actions than did their novice counterparts. Thus, procedural knowledge is, by its nature, more complex than is declarative knowledge; it is geared to solving problems (Anderson, 2005; Smith, 1995).

It seems that both the gifted and the expert research suggest that effective solving of complex problems requires the solver to focus on underlying action-based principles that direct problem solving. It appears that gifted students will be intellectually able to handle this kind of thinking before the other students in your class. Moreover, general thinking skills instruction is not always useful to gifted learners. Once a student knows something well, problem-solving skills become very domain-specific, and the skills become inextricably linked to content that is organized around procedural information. In successful gifted instruction, procedural knowledge and problem-solving skills are focused around achieving a domain-specific goal.

Problem Solving

IS IT A PROBLEM?

One issue with problem solving is that the term does not have an agreed-upon definition in cognitive psychology. However, because the curriculum presented in this book grows out of models of complex problem solving, an understanding of the term is integral to implementing the units. Therefore, I will discuss issues surrounding the definition of problem solving and proffer the definition that underlies the units.

In 1960, Newell, Shaw, and Simon—pioneers in the problem-solving research—wrote that "imperfect knowledge about how to proceed is at the core of the genuinely problematic" (p. 257). Although this seems straightforward, Reitman (1965), who moved problem-solving research into complex, open-ended areas, critiqued Newell et al.'s definition as too limited. Reitman preferred to say that a person "has a problem when [he or she] has been given a description of something but does not yet have anything that satisfies the description" (p. 126). Reitman's view is significantly different from Newell et al.'s in that it allows us to speak of how much difficulty a problem presents, rather than to draw "some arbitrary line between the trivial and the 'genuinely problematic'" (Reitman, 1965, p. 130). This distinction is central to my understanding of problems—particularly complex ones. The definition of a challenging problem is not so much categorical: Is it a hard or an easy problem? Rather, the definition falls along a continuum that could be labeled "how difficult is this problem?" Thus, when developing a project, I find it better to discuss degrees of difficulty—how hard students will find particular aspects of the problem are—rather than try to decide if students will find it a hard problem or not.

In many ways, complexity is the relationship between the problem and the solver. This is reminiscent of complexity in reading, where difficulty is not solely a characteristic of a text but the relationship of what the reader and author bring to the text. Therefore, what is complex for one student may not be complex for another—whether we are talking about a problem or a book.

Anderson (2005) and Glass and Holyoak (1986) listed the defining characteristics of a problem situation. According to Anderson, problem solving is always goal-directed behavior. It requires continually decomposing the original goal into narrower subgoals. Ultimately, subgoals are reached that can be achieved by direct actions. The affective solver then applies a series of actions (either mentally or physically) that will achieve the goals. Here, Sternberg (1997) would add that coordinating problem-solving behaviors falls under an executive function that keeps behaviors goal-directed. All units in this book grow out of the problem-solving literature and are presented as complex problems that require such cognitive effort to refine and solve.

WHAT MAKES A PROBLEM DIFFICULT?

Background knowledge. If you think of reading with comprehension as a complex problem, then it becomes understandable that difficulty, as Simon (1973, 1978) and Wenke and Frensch (2005) explained, is not an absolute, innate to the problem. Rather, the level of difficulty characterizes the relationship between problem solvers' preexisting knowledge and, possibly, intellectual ability and the given problem (Wenke & Frensch, 2005). According to the Kintsch and van Dyke (Kintsch & van Dyke, 1983; Weaver, Mannes, & Fletcher, 1995) reading model, much of the information needed to understand a text is not provided in the text itself, but must be drawn from the reader's (i.e., the problem solver's) prior knowledge. One example of this, drawn from the writings of E. D. Hirsch, Jr. (2006), is the sentence: "Jones sacrificed and knocked in a run." To understand the sentence about Jones, you have to know a lot about baseball that isn't explained: that a sacrifice is an intentional out, that at least one man must have been on base for it to occur, that this man made it home, and so on.

The implications of the role that content knowledge plays in a student's understanding of a text—or any content-rich problem—is massive: things not stated in the text or problem statement, but drawn from the student's memory are just as important as knowledge that is stated. Therefore, as I prepared units for this book, I had to determine how much content will be presented to the students, how much I can assume they know, and how much they will have to discover on their own during the project. I often left the decision about what information students are given and what they must discover on their own to either the teacher or to the students themselves.

Gifted children are more apt to develop elaborate associations within their knowledge bases (Butterfield & Ferretti, 1987). Therefore, each unit's culminating project is presented as a problem, and each solution requires mastery of factual, content components that are connected by cause-and-effect principles. These principles often are specific to the content area at hand.

I have thus far discussed the cognitive resources that gifted children bring to problems. I followed this with a discussion of the interaction between the student and the problem. Before presenting the units, I would like to discuss two more topics: what in the problem's structure adds to its difficulty and whether or not there is a difference between expert and gifted problem solvers.

WHAT MAKES ILL-STRUCTURED PROBLEMS UNIQUE?

Many cognitive psychologists (e.g., Davidson, 2003; Newell, 1969; Reitman, 1965) have distinguished between problems for which the path to the solution is evident and problems for which the problem solver finds this path to be incomplete and open-ended. The former set is referred to as well-structured and the latter set as ill-structured. For example, if an intellectually challenging algebra problem contains all the needed variables for solving it, and the student knows the best algorithms to reach the solution, the problem is considered well-structured. If, however, a problem were to require innovative thinking, demand that the student define some aspects before starting, and has a variety of solution paths, then the problem would be considered ill-structured.

Reitman's (1965) study of a composer creating a fugue is generally cited as the seminal work in ill-structured problem solving. According to Newell (1969), Reitman took the abstraction of a problem to be {X, =>, Y} where X is the information given for the problem statement (in our case, the assignment), => is the way to make changes in the problem space, and Y is the desired solution. Open constraints or options can be localized in any of these three aspects. The more open constraints that exist in each of these areas, the more ill-structured the problem. This simple mathematic representation of ill-structured problems drives all of the curricular units I develop because complexity can occur in only these three places. I have renamed them below, however, because discussing them in algebraic terms becomes cumbersome. Thus, in all the units, I consider how challenging to make each of the following aspects:

- **Presentation (X):** How is the problem presented? Here I decide how much initial structure and information to give the students and how much they will need to supply themselves.
- **Process (=>):** What cognitive processes will students have to engage to solve the problem? Here I decide what kinds of relationships students will have to establish among the pieces of information, to what depth, and through which learning styles.
- **Product (Y):** What will be the criteria for defining the solution? Here I decide how much students can define for themselves, what are the presentation options, and what is the evaluation rubric.

For the most part (but clearly, not always), I have found gifted learners enjoy ill-structured project parameters in ways that flummox more typical students. Moreover, I sometimes feel that defining an ill-structured problem statement is a significant part of the thought process for gifted students. Recently, I worked for 4 months on an interdisciplinary project with an amazing group of fifth-grade girls who were talented in science, language arts, and/or technology. At the initial meeting, my instructions took less than a minute: "I have this idea to make a movie in which Dr. Vieth, our superintendent, has a fatal disease that doctors cannot cure, but you, being highly knowledgeable, figure out how to shrink down, go inside her body, and save her." (OK, I got the idea from an old Raquel Welch movie, but they didn't know that.) Long story short, on the last day of school, the entire fifth grade gathered in the learning center to see the 10-part podcast that was reminiscent of old-time movie serials, but with a lot more content.

This was a perfect example of an ill-structured problem. The opening statement was very incomplete, taking over a month to define the problem to a point where they could start writing. There were countless ways (solution paths) to get to the ending. Moreover, the goal state was continually changing and evolving up until the last week.

The ill-structured problems at the core of the units in this book will require students to engage a creative approach to articulate the goals, turn them into coordinated subgoals, and reach a solution. This kind of intellectual behavior has been cited as one of the hallmarks of giftedness (English, 1992; Hoh, 2008; Sternberg & Davidson, 1986).

GIFTED OR EXPERT BEHAVIOR?

The field's understanding of expertise and its acquisition is relatively well documented. The field's understanding of the role intelligence plays in that acquisition is not. Across content areas, as a person acquires expertise, the knowledge available to deal with problems becomes (a) more related to the expert's particular content area, (b) more elaborated, and (c) more centered around goal-directed procedures. Moreover, problem-solving skills also become more specific to the content area and less generally applicable to a wide variety of problems. One fairly effective general strategy, for example, is to reduce differences between the initial state and the goal state. For instance, if you were hungry, obtaining food as fast as possible might be a workable plan that follows this general strategy. If you were to have expert knowledge of nutrition principles, however, you would use content-specific information to find a solution: the nutritional content, the influence of white flour on blood sugar, deleterious effects of ingesting pesticides, an understanding of a balanced diet—of course, all of this could go out the window if the dessert menu were a good one. The problem becomes more complicated just by the nature of the expert's knowledge base. Here, understanding the effects of certain foods on the body changes the problem from mere satiation to one with subgoals related to nutrition and economics. The units in this book are presented to move students toward this kind of content-rich, problem-solving style of thinking.

This brings us to the fact that contemporary views of cognition remain divided on the big question: "Are expert problem solvers people who are intellectually gifted, or is expertise available to anyone who puts in the practice time?" Many factors make finding an answer to the question a complex problem in itself.

First, the difficulties in answering this question are exacerbated by the fact that experts in a field tend to be people who have a proclivity in that field in the first place. This means that many of the subjects in expert studies might have begun with intellectual strengths related to success in the area being observed. Therefore, separating out the role IQ and talent plays in expertise becomes difficult.

Second, expertise is definable in a broad sense as mastery of a given domain at a given time with experts being the best performers in their respective fields (e.g., the athletes in Williams' [2002] study). Within various content areas, however, the definitions of "best performance" may be very different. Olympic skaters who are considered experts, for example, strive to perform certain aspects of their routines exactly the same way in each competition. A Pulitzer Prize-winning author, in contrast, whose books are strikingly similar, would not be considered an expert for very long. Although winning either prize would be a major achievement and require amazing talent, there appears to be a creative factor that is unique only to the latter situation. Perhaps when the achievement requires that the expert combine information in a novel way, intelligence plays a different kind of role.

Finally, although it seems counterintuitive, the research supporting the belief that a higher IQ translates to a better ability to solve complex problems is both slight and inconclusive. Further exacerbating the debate is the fact the most often cited study on this topic—a Sim City-like computer simulation conducted by

Dörner and his associates (e.g., Dörner, Kreuzig, Reither, & Stäudel, 1983)—had many variables, but did not require the solver to have a rich, principle-centered content knowledge base. In most domains, this kind of knowledge background is integral to what it means to be an expert. (If this issue were easy for us to understand, we wouldn't need to be gifted ourselves. Or are we just experts who have spent a lot of time in our fields?)

At best, other studies have only shown a modest correlation between general intelligence and complex problem solving. Such studies, however, have been criticized for small samples, methodological problems, or definitional issues. Therefore, the question of a relationship between general intelligence and problem-solving ability remains open (Wenke & Frensch, 2003).

Some people, and I am one of them, see problem solving as inseparable from intelligence. For these people, there is a creative component that goes beyond expert problem solving, requiring a highly developed intellect. Feldhusen (2005) wrote that giftedness, expertise, and creativity are inextricably linked concepts. Feldhusen (2005) explained that according to Gardner (1993), expertise is high-level, domain-specific mastery of procedural knowledge and problem-solving strategies. To Gardner, expertise is "a prelude to creative production" but creative thinking (i.e., the defining and solving of ill-defined problems) exceeds expert understanding. Gardner (1993) defined a very creative person as one who "solves problems, fashions products, or poses new questions in a domain in a way that is accepted within at least one cultural group" (p. 35).

Understanding the interrelationships among problem solving, intellect, and creativity may enable us to establish classrooms in which students can develop their talents to full fruition. Moreover, this idea that expertise is a prelude to high-level, creative achievement is integral to the units included in this book. That is, the units are designed to guide students to organize their knowledge around principles and to use this knowledge to define and solve complex problems.

The next and final section of this chapter will detail the structure of the units, explaining how they are designed to provide the intellectual stimulation needed for talented students to set their own goals and to strive for creative achievement. In short, the units will help you help your gifted students to bring their talents to fruition and their thinking to complexity.

Chapter Structure

This chapter has presented an overview of the thinking processes in which gifted students engage—an introduction for teachers new to developing gifted curriculum and additional ways to think about gifted thinking for those with experience. In connecting the information processing and gifted research together, I have tried to create an understanding of gifted students that might not be evident when we look at these two areas as distinct from each other. In developing the following chapters, I have drawn from this combined research strategies to challenge students in ways that are commensurate with a full range of their unique abilities.

Each remaining chapter will present a content-area unit. I have structured these units so that teachers can use them as lesson plans—each one is easily adaptable to grade-level and topic variations. All of the units are presented in six sections, with additional sections as needed:

1. **Overview:** The first section of each unit begins with a narrative overview that includes a summary of both the whole-class project and the gifted extension. This summary presents the content, process, and product/assessment goals.

2. **The Cognitive Connection:** The second section is a brief discussion of how the unit challenges and promotes the unique intellectual gifts of your students. It is the explanation of how the unit activities nurture the kinds of intellectual behaviors discussed above.

3. **National Standards:** All units have been designed to meet national standards and, when appropriate, 21st Century Skills. The specific standards and skills are listed here.

4. **Activities:** The fourth section presents a day-by-day schedule for the unit. However, "a day" is more of a concept than a class period. I think of a day as a step that should take a class period but, depending on the reactions of the students, may be a slightly less or more than a day. Each daily lesson includes homework assignments that can easily be given during class time or for independent work during study hall or library periods. At the end of the lesson you will find all of the handouts needed for the project. Feel free to copy and distribute them for educational purposes as you wish.

5. **Challenging Minds: Highlighted Activities:** This section highlights the activities that have been presented in the unit that can be used as self-contained activities in a variety of classrooms.

6. **Adaptations:** You know your students best and the units are designed for easy adaptation for a variety of classes or junior high grades. This final section suggests simple ways for you to adapt the units to the needs of your class. This may be ways you adjust for small-group or whole-class implementations, alternative texts, creative extensions, or truncating or expanding a lesson.

For students to experience success that matters to them, the curriculum needs to accommodate individual differences in intellectual talent and developmental level (Stevenson & Stigler, 1992). Achieving this goal with gifted students presents unique challenges. I am hopeful that this book will provide content-rich units that will make this goal more easily obtainable—that you can use the units to challenge your students and to develop their cognitive gifts.

Chapter 3

A Mystery Writing Project

Writing is thinking on paper.

—William Zinsser

Overview

These next two chapters contain complementary writing projects. This chapter introduces students to the expert writing model called knowledge transformation as they create a mystery. The next one develops the model further as students keep journals or blogs as if they were minor characters in William Golding's novel *Lord of the Flies*.

The primary focus of this unit is on developing strong personalities for the main characters. These personalities, in turn, then influence all of the other aspects of the story as students write a mystery. Because of this focus on character, some students who are not usually recognized as strong writers, but who have an insight into interpersonal behaviors, often blossom in this project.

The unit takes about a month, meeting three times a week. All of the students in the class receive the same introductory instruction during the first part of the unit. About halfway through, they are divided into small groups according to their writing talents. The second part of the unit is then devoted to story writing and peer editing. During this half, all students in the class are encouraged to develop intricate personalities for their main characters and to have these personalities play out in both subtle and obvious ways. If, for example, the student writes about someone who is selfish, this influences how that character might respond when paying a check or interacting with the detective. If the character is compulsively neat, this might affect how she inspects a crime scene or organizes her room.

Before beginning to draft, students work simultaneously on two problems: one devoted to establishing a character's personality and the other to establishing the structure (or schema) of the mystery. To establish character, students partake in several short writing activities, including creating bubble maps, writing descriptions of the character's home and car, and bringing in samples of items that the character might own. At the same time, students are analyzing examples of the genre for defining elements. I have taught the same unit, lesson for lesson, with other genres. Regardless of story type, it is characterization, rather than plot, that drives the writing. By the time students are in eighth grade, and participating in the next chapter's writing project (see Chapter 4), they are using a more complicated set of literary elements to constrain their storyline. These include character, setting, mood, and Freudian symbolism.

The Cognitive Connection

The problem-solving research presents two models of writing (Bereiter, Burtis, & Scardamalia, 1988; Smith, 1995): the knowledge telling model, usually employed by beginners, and the knowledge transformation model, usually employed by experts. The knowledge telling model can be seen as primarily local. Students begin by taking cues from either the assignment or an understanding of the genre at hand to generate their first sentences. These sentences then provide cues for the next segment. This linking of text segments continues throughout the entire text-construction process. Students who operate under this model typically stop when they have completed the requisite number of pages or when the final segment offers no more cues for further content. It is basically a think it/write it model.

According to the knowledge telling model, beginning writers tend to create oversimplified, shallow problem representations of the writing task. When constructing these representations, they usually spend more time on lower level goals, give themselves few guidelines, and do little self-monitoring or advanced planning. Expert writers, in contrast, develop plans around rhetorical and genre schemata that they instantiate with goals and content unique to the assignment. Such schemata are used not only for structuring the content, but also for maintaining an overall focus, a sense of reader, and for developing a main point in depth. In contrast to the linear production of the knowledge telling model, the knowledge transformation model posits an iterative process in which text is generated through constraints that influence both content and genre knowledge. Throughout this unit, students are guided to use these constraints to define and integrate subgoals that include (a) revealing and maintaining characters' personalities and (b) detailing a setting that illustrates characters' personalities.

If the teacher's task were simply to make students efficient writers, then the beginner model would be sufficient. Schools could train students to apply this model and assume that better writers will, given their talents, shift to the expert model through repeated writing challenges. However, this chapter provides direct instruction that will foster these students' metacognitive awareness for applying the knowledge transformation model. The next chapter reinforces this awareness, but increases the number of constraints that students need to maintain when generating text. This direct instruction potentially benefits all students in the classroom, but is particularly valuable to gifted writers who can readily transition to the more complex model with the right instruction.

According to the Rhode Island Gifted Association (n.d.), many gifted students learn basic skills quickly and with less practice than their age peers. They also have well-developed powers of conceptualization and synthesis. Moreover, they have a keen awareness of cause and effect, as well as other kinds of abstract complexities. Because of this early ability to deal with abstract, verbal complexities, linguistically gifted students are often able to implement procedures associated with the knowledge transformation model at a young age.

To respond to these characteristics in talented writers, I have developed Chapters 3 and 4 to encourage these writers to transition into the knowledge transformation model at a young age. Students are introduced to the model in this chapter and to a more elaborate version in the next one.

Developing Characters

Some writers will claim that setting drives their writing. For them, decisions about action depend on where the characters are. For me, character drives writing. I begin my own pieces of fiction with character profiles so that I will know how the characters will respond to events, what their surroundings will look like, and how they will interact with each other. One of my published short stories is therefore used as a model in the instruction for this project. If students can develop such an understanding of how character can drive story elements, then they are beginning to employ the overriding goals to monitor their own writing. This use of overriding goals that guide text production is a defining strategy essential of the knowledge transformation model.

National Standards

FROM THE INTERNATIONAL READING ASSOCIATION AND NATIONAL COUNCIL OF TEACHERS OF ENGLISH (1996):

- Students read a wide range of literature from many periods in many genres to build an understanding of the many dimensions (e.g., philosophical, ethical, aesthetic) of human experience.
- Students apply a wide range of strategies to comprehend, interpret, evaluate, and appreciate texts. They draw on their prior experience, their interactions

with other readers and writers, their knowledge of word meaning and of other texts, their word identification strategies, and their understanding of textual features (e.g., sound-letter correspondence, sentence structure, context, graphics).

- Students adjust their use of spoken, written, and visual language (e.g., conventions, style, vocabulary) to communicate effectively with a variety of audiences and for different purposes.

- Students employ a wide range of strategies as they write and use different writing process elements appropriately to communicate with different audiences for a variety of purposes.

- Students apply knowledge of language structure, language conventions (e.g., spelling and punctuation), media techniques, figurative language, and genre to create, critique, and discuss print and nonprint texts.

OBJECTIVES

Students will:

1. Write a mystery that has the following genre characteristics:
   - crime
   - detective
   - clues
   - suspect/motivation

2. Create a strong character before beginning to draft the story.
3. Reveal the personality through things the character does, says, and has.
4. Create a setting that reflects character.
5. Use symbolism to reflect the character's personality.
6. Engage in peer editing.

Lesson 1: Characteristics of Characters

PROCEDURE

1. **Explain** that the class is about to begin a unit on mystery writing. Ask what they think will be most important to their story: plot, character, or setting. (Discuss all answers.) Explain that for this project, students, as some professional authors do, are going to focus on character before plot, and that this should help make their stories more interesting.

2. **Ask** who they think is the most interesting character on TV or in movies. List the names of the suggested characters on the board. Discuss why students find these characters interesting. Have students vote for their favorite, but do not erase the remaining names.

3. **Pick** one of the final names that seems particularly familiar. Begin a bubble map of the character's personality by writing the name at the top of the board in a circle. Draw another circle under the name and connect the two circles with a line. Write "personality" in this new circle. Elicit three words, such as "studious," "ethical," and "loyal," that describe the character's personality. Write these inside the second circle under "personality."

4. **Draw** three lines radiating from the "personality" circle. Ask the class to think of something the character owns (e.g., a report card with all A's), says frequently (e.g., "I have to study"), or has done (e.g., completed her experiment first) that shows these personality traits. Write each example at the end of one of the lines.

5. **Have** students work in pairs to make a similar personality bubble map for one of the other characters on the list. They should have at least six lines radiating from the personality circle.

6. **Ask** students to read what they have written but not say the character's name or the central personality traits. Other students should guess who the character is from the shared clues.

7. **Discuss** the following questions about how an author reveals a character's personality:

   - How do authors let you know a character's personality? (Through what the character does, says, or has.)
   - What if the author just tells you the word that describes the personality? Is this just as effective? (Discuss all answers.)
   - Does a character need a certain personality in a story? (Discuss all answers.)

8. **Explain** that for some authors, personality is more important than plot. Ask if anyone agrees or disagrees. (Discuss all answers.) Ask if they have given much thought to the personalities of characters about whom they have

written about in the past. Reiterate that creating strong characters for their mysteries will be a major focus of this project.

HOMEWORK

Students may choose one of the following activities:

- Develop a bubble map for another character in literature (e.g., the wicked queen in *Snow White* or Malfoy in *Harry Potter*) that will be well known to their classmates. Use at least six details that show the personality.
- Make a collage of the personality of a character from literature by using words and pictures cut out of magazines.

Lesson 2: Show, Don't Tell

PROCEDURE

1. **Have** students meet in small groups and share their homework. Collect and grade the homework, if you wish.

2. **Explain** that one goal of this project is to have students *show* personality rather than stating a summary word that *tells* it. Instead of writing that a character is "kind" or "mean," better writers will create a scene showing the character's personality.

3. **Have** a student read aloud the first three paragraphs on page 26 of J. K. Rowling's (2002) *Harry Potter and the Goblet of Fire*. Discuss the following questions:

   - What are the contrasting ways in which the Dursleys treat Harry and Dudley when Harry enters the room? (They ignore Harry, and fuss over Dudley.)
   - How do they feel about Dudley? (They ignore his flaws and think he is gifted.)
   - How do you know which boy they like better if the author doesn't tell you? (By the things the Dursleys do.)
   - Does the author also need to state explicitly that the Dursleys prefer Dudley? Would it make their feelings clearer? (Discuss all answers.)
   - How does this passage model how an author shows various characters' personalities in a way that you might use in your own writing? (I could have characters do things to reveal their feelings and personality rather than by using words that summarize their feelings or by only telling the plot events.)

4. **Explain** that the challenge for good writers is to keep showing personality as they have the events in the story unfold, not to do one or the other. This will become more evident as the project continues.

5. **Reinforce** this concept of "showing, not telling," by having students read the description of Harry Potter's room on page 38 of J. K. Rowling's (2005) *Harry Potter and the Half Blood Prince*. Discuss why the author does not need to conclude with a statement that the room is sloppy.

6. **Read** the following student sample aloud and explain that it is a model for the homework:

   > I noticed that his hair was combed to the side perfectly so no one could see the bald spot on top of his head. When we had finished, he didn't offer to pay. I said, "Well, that was nice. Maybe we could do it again." He then looked at his Rolex and said, "Well, I don't know because I'm very busy and I have more important things to

do than socialize." And then he walked away without even saying goodbye. (Lindsay M.)

7. **Discuss** the piece using the following questions:
   - What are some traits that describe the personality of the main character in this passage? (arrogance, vanity, aloofness)
   - What is something that the character does to show these traits? (covers his bald spot, refuses to pay)
   - What items does he have that show his personality? (a perfect part in his hair, a Rolex)
   - What does he say that helps indicate his personality? (He is busy with important things.)

HOMEWORK

Students should complete the following:

Write a paragraph similar to the sample given in class. It should be about two people eating breakfast. Through what the characters do, say, or have, reveal how they feel about each other, but do not use any words that summarize their feelings. In the story, underline one thing a character had, one thing the character does, and one thing the character says that reveals the personality trait being shown.

Lesson 3: Jackets Have Personalities and No One Drives Just a Car

PROCEDURE

1. **Have** two students read their stories written for homework to the class. Have other students respond to the shared pieces using the following critiquing guidelines:
   - The first two comments should be on specific things that the writer did well (e.g., "I liked the way you used a lot of objects that showed personality").
   - Comments such as "I liked it" or "It was good" should be followed by a teacher's prompt of "What specifically did you like about it?" or "What in the piece made you think it was good?"
   - The third comment should be introduced by the teachers with the following, "An author can always add something that could make a piece even better. What might the author have added or done differently that would help you see the character's personalities even more clearly?"

2. **Collect** and grade the homework, if you wish.

3. **Explain** that one thing that sets better writers apart from others is that they rarely use general nouns like "jacket" or "car." Instead they replace these kinds of nouns with specific ones that suggest the character's personality. This use of specific nouns will be the focus of this lesson.

4. **Share** pictures of three very different jackets. (I always show a worn leather biker jacket, a black Burberry trench coat, and a leather dress coat with a large fur collar.)

5. **Have** students discuss the different personalities that are suggested by each one.

6. **Have** students work with partners to write a sentence or two that reflects something the owner of one of the jackets might say. Have students read their sentences aloud. Then have others students guess which one of the jackets the authors had in mind.

7. **Ask** what else the character might own or what the character might have been doing when wearing the jacket.

8. **Explain** that a person can have more than one personality trait and own two or three of these jackets, but for the purposes of a short story, authors do not usually create characters with this kind of complexity. This is because when publishing a short story, length is almost always a constraint. It is therefore difficult to develop several traits in one story. A character can have an experience that changes his or her personality, however.

9. **Explain** that not every character would drive the same car. One character might drive a safe car, such as a Volvo, but a different character who disdains other people might ride in the back of a limo with the partition raised.

HOMEWORK

Students should complete the following:

Students should start thinking about the central personality trait of the main characters they wish to use in their mysteries and they should complete the following story using that character as the subject:

> S/He was late for a job interview and the job was important. S/He rushed to take off in the _____ (car) and, without looking, sideswiped a dog.

Tell students that they should have some storyline that shows a personality consistent with the car. Or as David B., one of my students, put it, "keep the story going while you show the character." Students may rewrite the introduction to better fit the mood of their piece. Read the following student example to the class for inspiration:

> He got into his semi-truck that was littered with empty Cheetos bags and had a dent right in the middle of the grill. He was late for the job interview. He wasn't paying attention and he sideswiped a dog. He bounced up in his seat not knowing what had happened, but he was late and the Cheetos were giving him a headache. He just kept on driving. (Sean F.)

Lesson 4: Mary Gorney

PROCEDURE

1. **Have** several students read their homework pieces from the previous lesson. Use the critiquing guidelines from the previous lesson to elicit responses to the pieces that were read aloud.

2. **Explain** that a symbolic object represents an aspect of a person's life or personality. For example, an actor might have a showy piece of jewelry that commands attention or a rock star may have a special tattoo. They will see examples of these objects in the story that they are about to hear.

3. **Read** aloud the beginning of the short story that I had published in *Cricket* Magazine (Smith, 2000). (See Handout 1 at the end of this unit.) Explain that the story is about a young boy who lives in a blue-collar neighborhood. His next-door neighbor is an older woman named Mary Gorney. As students are listening to the story, they should try to pick out several symbolic objects from the story. They also should think about how objects represent the characters' personalities and lives.

4. **Ask** students what symbolic objects were used in the story and what these objects reveal about the characters. If students do not discuss the following objects, be sure to ask students what they think the author was trying to suggest by mentioning them:

   - **The brown brick rectangular houses:** This symbolizes the type of neighborhood in which the story takes place. The houses are not fancy and all look similar.
   - **Mary Gorney's closed windows:** This was symbolic for her wanting to keep people out of her house, or maybe she was closed to making new friends.
   - **The webbed aluminum chairs that people used to sit around their front steps:** These also symbolize the economic status of the neighborhood. This shows that people were friendly with each other because they all were sitting outside at the same time.
   - **Mary's night work:** This shows she was different from the rest of the neighbors who were all sitting outside while she was at work.

5. **Ask** the class to work together to generate a bubble map of Mary Gorney's personality. On the board, place her name in the center of a circle with three secondary circles labeled "has," "says," and "does"; tertiary bubbles should state specific examples of each of these. Have students make up other things that she might have, say, or do that would be consistent with her personality.

6. **Have** students work independently to make bubble maps on their own main character. Under the character's name, students should write the central personality trait. Some students might choose to write a second trait, as

well. (I always tell students that their main character needs to be about their own age and that the crime and setting need to be familiar to them, so their stories cannot be about adult jewel thieves in Paris.)

The main problem that students have had with successfully creating these maps has with been being consistent across the personality traits that they wrote on the bubble map; students tend to list creative items, but the items do not reflect a unifying trait. When creating his map and description, one student, Drew C., turned in a list that had items such a ripped backpack, a blue bike, a winter coat with a broken zipper, and a lunch bag that didn't fit in his backpack. Although these items were creative and items that a sixth grader would own, they didn't have a unifying theme that said anything about the character as a person. When given a chance to do the assignment over, he came up with this list: encyclopedias that he has read from A–Z, thousands of medals for his academic achievement, all A's on his report card, a Harvard sweatshirt, and a watch with 20 functions. After reading this list of five items, you could gather that this character is smart.

7. **Have** students use these personality traits to write a paragraph that describes the bedroom of their main character. Explain that this paragraph will be integrated into their final mystery. Remind them to be sure to include examples of "says," "has," and "does." The objects that the person has should say a great deal about the character's life. Read aloud the following student examples of this assignment:

> He went over to his dresser and reached into his third drawer, "the blue drawer." He put on his blue "book" pajamas and went to bed. He fell asleep solving math equations in his head. (J. T. T.)

> Beauty Nelsie walked into her bedroom and sat on her silver monogrammed bedspread. She traced the B with her hand and said, "Beautiful, just beautiful." (Mary L.)

> My closet has a space for everything. I hang all of my clothes except for my socks—each type of clothing is organized in rainbow order with red on the left and black on the right. (Jordon B.)

HOMEWORK
Students should complete the following:
   Finish the description of the character's room.

Lesson 5: Writing Summaries

PROCEDURE

1. **Ask** several students to share their paragraphs.
2. **Use** the critiquing guidelines from Lesson 3 to elicit responses to the pieces that were read aloud. Have classmates comment on the following questions when responding to the pieces that were read aloud.
   - What single trait was the author trying to show throughout the paragraph?
   - How did the author reveal this trait?
   - Did the use of symbolic objects help you to understand the trait?

3. **Give** students the following choices for how they will use their class time for the remainder of the session:
   - Rewrite their descriptions or maps.
   - Write a three-paragraph summary of their plot. (Remember, plots have to deal with situations and characters that are familiar to them—no diamond thefts or kidnappings.)

4. **Collect** and grade the bedroom descriptions and bubble maps, if you wish.

HOMEWORK

Students should complete the following:

Finish the three-paragraph plot summary.

Lesson 6: Reading and Drafting

PROCEDURE

1. **Explain** that the objective for today's class is to start writing the first draft of the mystery, but before beginning, students are going to read a famous mystery. Ask students to list at least three things they already know about the story just by the fact that it is a mystery. (Discuss students' answers. Responses generally fall into three categories: (a) responses indicating they are unsure; (b) general literature responses such as it will have a plot or a problem; and (c) genre-specific responses such as it will have a crime, a detective, or clues.) Explain that as the project progresses, they may be surprised by how much they already know that will prove useful in their writing.

2. **Have** students read or listen to you read aloud the first paragraph of "The Red-Headed League," one of Arthur Conan Doyle's favorites of all his Sherlock Holmes stories. A printable copy of the story and a blog for students' comments can be found at http://www.eastoftheweb.com/short-stories/UBooks/RedHead.shtml. Use the following question to have students discuss the introduction:
   - The author begins with an interaction between Holmes and Watson. Why might he have begun this way? (He wanted to establish their personalities in the beginning.)
   - What does this interaction show about each character's personality? (Watson is very polite. Holmes is excited and aggressive. Holmes is probably in charge because he directs the action.)
   - Because it is a mystery, what do you already know about the story? (There is probably a crime, and the detective will find clues and solve it. There may be several suspects.)

3. **Read** the rest of the story aloud to the class.
4. **Discuss** the story using the following questions:
   - Early on, Holmes mentions that he has been involved in thousands of cases. Why does the author have him say this? (To show that Holmes thinks of himself as an expert.)
   - What does the description of Wilson say about him? (He is very plain. The author highlights his red hair.)
   - What are some of the things Homes figures out about Wilson from the man's appearance? What does Holmes' ability to figure out these details instantly say about the detective's personality? (For example, from the larger size of Wilson's right hand, Holmes figures out that Wilson does manual labor. This rapid discerning of the clues shows that Holmes is very smart.)
   - What word summarizes Holmes's key trait? (Smart)

- How does Holmes reveal his personality throughout the story? (He asks important questions about what appear to be minor details. He wants to see classical music—Sarasate was a classical violinist of the time. He has "exact knowledge of London.")
- What clues does Holms use to solve the crime? (Clay's wrinkled and stained pants suggested digging, the hollow sound when he tapped the pavement, the location of the pawn shop and the bank)

5. **Explain** that there are two kinds of mysteries. In the first, which this story illustrates, there is one suspect and the detective has to figure out how the suspect has committed the crime. In the other, there are several suspects and the detective has to figure out which one is guilty. Students may use either kind for their own story.

6. **Review** the following story guidelines:
   - **Sustain the character throughout the whole story:** Most people can establish a character's personality. It is difficult, however, to maintain and show the personality throughout the story. Tell students that whenever they begin a new event, they should always ask themselves, "How would a person who is _____ (fill in personality trait) do this?" Stress the idea of sustaining the character throughout the whole story. For example, if the character starts out as a messy person, don't have him lose that character trait halfway through the story. **Reinforce** this point with the following role-play game:
     - Write the following words on separate slips of paper and place them in an empty cup: shy, cool, self-important, friendly, sneaky.
     - Have a student pick one of the personality types out of the cup and pretend to walk into the room late in the style of the word. Have other students guess the word from the way that the actor presents the event.
     - Repeat this same activity with other words drawn from the cup.
     - Remind students that this game is similar to the lesson on jackets and cars. Almost everything a character does in the story should be influenced by the personality the author is trying to maintain. This is equally true for simple events such as entering a room or major ones such as catching a suspect.

   - **No "lucking out":** The character can't just "get lucky" and find something that moves the plot forward (e.g., the missing baseball happens to be in the locker that the detective has randomly selected).
   - **No gaps:** The story can't just move from the grocery store to the police station; there needs to be an explanation of why the location has shifted.
   - **Show, don't tell:** The reader should be *shown* the characters' personalities.

7. **Assign** the students to writing groups.

> When teaching young writers to transition to the knowledge transformation model, I prefer to group students homogeneously. This is because talented writers seem better able to integrate more constraints into their writing with less iteration than do their peers. Moreover, they tend to be more metacognitively aware of the model when writing and are able to give more complex feedback. As an alternative method of grouping students, Vopat (2009) suggested having students list classmates they think will help them become better writers and using these lists as the basis for grouping students.

8. **Have** students share their bubble map and plot summary with the group. In responding to the speaker, group members should use an abbreviated version of the critiquing guidelines, offering one positive comment and one suggestion for improvement. Specific comments about the plot summary should focus on how well the writer met the four story guidelines discussed above.

9. **Give** students three class periods to write their stories. (This can be adjusted depending on how much you wish students to write at home.)

HOMEWORK

Students should complete the following:

Work on story drafts.

Lessons 7 and 8: Peer Editing

PROCEDURE

1. **Have** students work with partners from their groups to review and comment on each other's drafts. (I often tell students to select a passage that they found particularly troublesome to read to their partner for comment, not the whole story.)

HOMEWORK

Students should complete the following:

Correct drafts for submission. (I sometimes have students underline the ways they show character throughout the story. This helps many of them monitor their continued use of "showing not telling" through what the character has, says, and does.)

Lesson 9: Sharing Stories

PROCEDURE

1. **Have** students share their stories with their groups or the entire class. Encourage other students to make positive comments about the characterizations and how these affect the story.

Conclusion

I have found that student writers generally fall into three categories. At the highest level are those whose text and writing process reveals a complete integration of the knowledge transformation model. These students sustain and continue to reveal characters' personalities throughout the story as they move the plot forward. This is the smallest segment of the class, and although it includes many of the students who had previously been identified as "talented" writers, it often includes students whose writing suddenly shines with this assignment. David, for example, a student who had long been identified as talented in areas such as math and science, but not writing, fell into this category. An excerpt from his writing follows:

> It was Monday morning, one hour before school, when Danny Armston rolled out of his bed and onto the floor, taking the fluffy cotton comforter with him. He awoke with a startled clump and dived back into bed as the clock struck 7. As he glanced up at the plain old white walls, he saw all of his 4th, 5th, and 6th grade report cards hanging from the ceiling, which reminded him of Show-and-Tell Day. Danny knew exactly what to bring. He got out of bed and walked over to his shelves that held every project, test, and homework assignment that he had ever completed. He grabbed something out of the first grade folder. In it was his Invention Convention certificate that he received for having the best Pine Wood Derby car in the first grade.
>
> After grabbing his certificate, he hurried over to the right side of his dresser that held his light colored clothes, unlike the left side that held the dark. Finally, he grabbed his science textbook, which was, of course, on his little desk tucked away in the back corner of his room. . . .
>
> Danny took out his white journal and jotted him down as a suspect. When he got home, he would rip out the page with the clues and put it in his detective folder on his shelf. Before he put it in the folder, he would cut off the hanging edges with scissors. (David B.)

The second, and largest, category appears to be a transition one between the two models. Students in this category seem to be attempting to develop characters' personalities, but it appears as if they are interrupting the plot to tell a particular character detail rather than having the characters carry out actions in ways that are in keeping with their personalities.

Finally, students in the third category seem unready to shift from knowledge telling to knowledge transformation. Although these students seem able to establish a character's personality in the beginning of the story, they soon drop any aspects of personality and reduce the character to a one-dimensional person whose purpose is to move the action forward.

Challenging Minds: Highlighted Activities

Following is a list of activities used in this unit that can be adapted to many instructional and enrichment situations to complement a variety of student strengths.

1. **Show and tell:** I often have students bring in items that might have belonged to an historical or fictional character. Usually, they are asked to discuss the relevance of the article in first person.

2. **Manner of the word:** The game where students act out small vignettes in the manner of the word is a novel way to teach adverbs. I have a student leave the room and the rest of the class picks an adverb (e.g., shyly, boldly, awkwardly). The student then returns and asks classmates to perform little activities—such as asking someone to borrow a pen or singing—in the manner of the word. This continues until the student can guess the adverb. Make the point that the same activity (i.e., verb) can be acted out differently depending on the adverb.

3. **Collage:** This project encourages students to think about fictional characters, historical figures, or people in the news from a visual/spatial perspective. There are many variations that can be used: placing the real personality in a central circle and the public persona on the outside, being color-specific to match the personality, placing two opposing characters on the same collage, and showing a character or person at two different points in life.

Adaptations

As stated in the introduction, using the mystery genre is not a requisite for implementing this project; any genre that your students are studying can be used. The knowledge transformation model is predicated on the idea that students are developing and coordinating genre characteristics and content at the same time. Therefore, as long as a particular genre is used and students are constrained by its characteristics, this project would need very little adaptation other than changing some of the suggested readings. I also like using suspense stories for this project; for some students, this is a less intellectually demanding genre and thus allows them to focus more attention on character.

When students are particularly adept at creating character, I have them describe more settings that complement the personalities being developed. I also ask them to expand the room description and we discuss how character and setting can combine to create mood. In short, I increase the number of subproblems that the writer needs to coordinate with in the piece. Think of the complexity of this project as a continuum of constraints ranging from one or two to multiple interacting constraints—as discussed in the next chapter.

Handout 1
Opening Pages of "Mary Gorney"
by Kenneth J. Smith ©

Our street was lined with rectangular, brown-bricked duplexes. Two joined houses, a driveway, two joined houses, a driveway, from one corner to the next. The homes on the right had stoops on the front. The ones on the left had stoops on the side.

On the other side of our driveway lived Mary Gorney. She was unlike everyone else on the street. The rest of us knew the history of all the families that came out of hibernation within the same few early spring days to set up webbed aluminum chairs around their stoops. But Mary Gorney kept to herself. On summer evenings, when all the windows and doors on the block were opened to catch the night breezes, hers were closed. It seemed as if no one else on the block even knew that she lived there.

She worked nights as a nurse. She was thin and tall, too tall for a woman. I hardly ever saw her except when I left late for school and she was coming home from work. Even so, if I heard her car as I was going out the door, I'd wait until she was inside before I'd leave. I figured being late was not nearly as bad as having Mary Gorney looking at me.

I spent my summers in the park at the end of the block next to the McMann's house—a small playground that I had outgrown and a large field. There were always kids there for a pick-up softball game in the afternoon or a basketball game after dinner.

One hot late-summer day there was no breeze. The tree outside my bedroom was wilted and still. The clouds were stacked in the sky. I began heading down the side stairs when my mother called me back into the house.

"Mary Gorney has been sick for a few days. Stop in and see if she needs anything before you go to the park."

"You want me to go inside old lady Gorney's house? No way."

"Don't argue with me. She's alone and has no one to help her. It won't kill you to help her."

"It might," I yelled back as I slammed the screen door. I looked over at her door. White, like ours. After crossing the driveways, I knocked, but got no answer. I knocked again and thought that I heard her say, "Come in." Opening the door slowly, I called out.

"Come in," she said again. I could hear a strain in her voice.

I walked through the kitchen and TV room into the living room. She was sitting in one of two low wooden chairs with blue-striped cushions. She was wearing a green robe that looked like it was made from a quilt. It was buttoned to the neck. She looked pale, even in her colored robe.

Looking around the room, I thought that everything was odd. The floors were not carpeted but shining wood. There were rugs with small blue and red patterns in front of the sofa and chairs. They looked like the ones in my book about Aladdin. None of the furniture had square corners. The tables were shaped like kidney beans.

"Your mother said that you'd come to help me. I'm sorry to keep you in on a nice day. I need my books packed up. They are coming to take them away and I can't pack them myself. I can pay you. You can have some of them, if you like."

I was sure my mother wouldn't let me take any money, especially from a lady who couldn't afford carpeting.

Chapter 4

A Freudian Analysis of Literature

When inspiration does not come to me, I go halfway to meet it.

—Sigmund Freud

Overview

In this unit, students study Sigmund Freud's psychoanalytic theory of the human personality. They then use this theory to analyze William Golding's classic, dark novel, *Lord of the Flies*. The novel chronicles the descent into savagery of a group of boys who are stranded on an island. By juxtaposing a world at war with the boy's island society, Golding suggests several themes related to the nature of human kind that mirror Freud's theory.

The Freudian aspects of this unit focus on the three interactive parts of the human personality: id, ego, and superego. More than defining these terms, the unit presents the merits and flaws of each aspect under complex circumstances and interactions. It is this complexity that segues students into the events of the novel, as well as important current and historic events. Ancillary aspects of Freud's theory, such as defense mechanisms and stages of development, also are explored in the project.

As stated, this project is centered on the novel, *Lord of the Flies*. It is presented, however, as a model of a psychology-based analysis of literature and several other novels would work just as well. I have at times, for example, done a follow-up unit based on Robert Louis Stevenson's *Strange Case of Dr. Jekyll and Mr. Hyde*, a much shorter work that could easily replace Golding's novel in the instruction. A list of other alternative works of varying complexity is proffered at the end of the daily lessons.

I have taught this particular novel to eighth graders more than 30 times and have rarely found a student who hasn't enjoyed it. It is this unit, more than any other, that keeps students after class to continue the daily discussions. The unit does include some atypical, creative aspects, but follows a more traditional, Socratic instructional method than do most of my units. This is because it is usually presented at the end of students' junior high careers as an introduction to the kinds of challenges that they can expect in their upcoming high-level high school classes.

The project begins with a discussion of core Freudian concepts and the historical context in which Freud lived. It runs approximately 6 weeks, with students meeting with me three times a week and working independently or in small groups once a week. During this 6 weeks, students keep journals or online blogs as minor characters in the story, and present a PowerPoint (or Keynote) slide show on an aspect of Freud's theory that I have not presented in the lectures. Moreover, they annotate the novel as they read, take a final exam, and present small-group or independent "mandatory/optional" projects. These projects are student-defined, but must show a creative extension of the content and themes of the project. For example, students have presented lawyers' closing arguments to a jury for a trial based on crimes committed on the island and campaign speeches the main character would give if he were to grow up and run for Prime Minster of England. Because so much of the instruction in this chapter follows a traditional style, a final exam and a grading sheet are included at the end of this chapter.

When I taught the unit in a Chicago-based private school for highly capable students, it was presented to the whole class. More typically, certain students are designated for participation in the unit, while the rest of the class reads a more grade-level appropriate book such as *The Diary of a Young Girl* by Anne Frank. In this latter scenario, at the end of the unit, all students come together to compare their experiences and share their insights into the themes related to the nature of humankind's potential.

The Cognitive Connection

Research on the writing process strongly indicates that one cognitive model describes the writing process of experts while a qualitatively different one describes the processes used by more ordinary writers. Some of this research has revealed this difference in writers as early as third grade. As discussed in Chapter 3, these models are the knowledge transformation model that experts tend to use and the knowledge telling model that beginners tend to use (Bereiter et al., 1988; Breetvelt, van den Bergh, & Rijlaarsdam, 1994; Smith, 1995). Briefly, writers who engage in the knowledge transformation model strive to coordinate and fulfill goals that are related to structure or genre with goals that are related to content. The coordination of these goals comes under the control of executive or high-level goals geared to produce a unified piece of writing.

All of the writing assignments present within these chapters lay the groundwork for students to engage in and internalize the knowledge transformation model. The previous chapter presented the first writing unit that I teach that is designed to explicitly guide young writers to engage in knowledge transformation throughout their writing. It provided a unit with a limited number of subgoals focused primarily on genre and character. This unit, which I usually teach to eighth graders, encourages students to employ a full-fledged, complex knowledge transformation model.

The primary fiction writing in this unit is the journal or blog. Students, assuming the role of a minor character in the story, write approximately five entries, each corresponding to a major event in the novel. They also respond in character to each other's entries.

For each entry, the assignment states the overriding goal that focuses and coordinates all the other goals. These other goals relate to genre and/or content. Each entry introduces new goals and repeats those introduced in the previous assignments. Thus, the first entry focuses on establishing a character and using imagery. By the time students reach the final entry, lessons have guided students to integrate goals including not only character and imagery, but also sustaining voice and symbolism; creating mood; and, perhaps most challenging, reflecting the role of id, ego, and superego through a variety of literary elements.

One sign of intellectually gifted thinkers is their ability to handle complex, principle-based thought before their peers can. The Freudian model of personality provides an opportunity for this kind of reasoning. I recently ran into Samantha, a ninth grader who had previously participated in this project. She told me that more than once her teachers told her class that they would enjoy learning about id and superego when they were seniors. It leaves the teachers nonplussed to hear her tell them that she studied it in eighth grade. This idea that Freudian psychology is beyond the grasp of junior high students also is reflected in the American Psychology Association's complete lack of standards for classes below high school. Yet, I have never found students who did not find it within their grasp of understanding. Memorizing the definition of terms such as id, ego, and defense mechanisms, no matter how complicated, is still simply retelling facts. Recognizing the interactions of the terms, as well as using them to justify interpretations and guide their annotating, raises students' understanding of principle-based knowledge. It is this understanding of principle-based knowledge that characterizes gifted learners and that is central to students' participation in this project.

Gifted students are taking in and processing more than do their same-age peers. They also integrate this new information relatively easily into their existing knowledge base to create a more complex representation of concepts. As research shows, when learning, they use more of their brain in processing information (Eide & Eide, 2004). This high-level processing results in more elaborate versions of their preexisting concept networks. Therefore, this unit is content rich and fast paced to challenge students in ways commensurate with their ability.

Finally, students' more complex understanding facilitates their solving of difficult intellectual problems. The intellectual problems presented here are typical of what will be expected of them in upper level high school classes. In this unit, however, students are guided to develop the intellectual structures they will be expected to have to respond to literature in these high school classes. Students learn to detail their opinions by beginning with a thesis statement and providing a variety of text-based and external support for the thesis. Moreover, students must use content to solve creative, novel problems when they develop their mandatory/optional projects and when they interpret the book's and Freud's themes. In short, this unit exemplifies ill-structured problem solving and provides the kinds of challenges that define gifted learners.

Edition Recommendation

For this unit, I have used the edition of *Lord of the Flies* published by Riverhead Books. It is a larger edition than others I have seen and is thus easier for students to annotate should they be able to write in their books. All page number references throughout the unit are from this edition. Other editions will work equally well, but should you use a different version from the recommended one, you will need to adjust this chapter's page number references accordingly. Should this be the case, I have referred to the events in the chapter so that you can easily find the passages being discussed.

National Standards

FROM THE AMERICAN PSYCHOLOGICAL ASSOCIATION (2005):
Students are able to:
- Describe the role of critical periods in development.
- Explain the role of personality constructs as a framework for organizing behavioral phenomena.
- Identify important contributions to the understanding of personality.

FROM THE INTERNATIONAL READING ASSOCIATION AND NATIONAL COUNCIL OF TEACHERS OF ENGLISH (1996):
- Students read a wide range of print and nonprint texts to build an understanding of texts, of themselves, and of the cultures of the United States and the world; to acquire new information; to respond to the needs and demands of society and the workplace; and for personal fulfillment. Among these texts are fiction and nonfiction, classic, and contemporary works.

- Students read a wide range of literature from many periods in many genres to build an understanding of the many dimensions (e.g., philosophical, ethical, aesthetic) of human experience.
- Students apply a wide range of strategies to comprehend, interpret, evaluate, and appreciate texts. They draw on their prior experience, their interactions with other readers and writers, their knowledge of word meaning and of other texts, their word identification strategies, and their understanding of textual features (e.g., sound-letter correspondence, sentence structure, context, graphics).
- Students adjust their use of spoken, written, and visual language (e.g., conventions, style, vocabulary) to communicate effectively with a variety of audiences and for different purposes.
- Students employ a wide range of strategies as they write and use different writing process elements appropriately to communicate with different audiences for a variety of purposes.
- Students apply knowledge of language structure, language conventions (e.g., spelling and punctuation), media techniques, figurative language, and genre to create, critique, and discuss print and nonprint texts.
- Students conduct research on issues and interests by generating ideas and questions, and by posing problems. They gather, evaluate, and synthesize data from a variety of sources (e.g., print and nonprint texts, artifacts, people) to communicate their discoveries in ways that suit their purpose and audience.
- Students use a variety of technological and information resources (e.g., libraries, databases, computer networks, video) to gather and synthesize information and to create and communicate knowledge.
- Students use spoken, written, and visual language to accomplish their own purposes (e.g., for learning, enjoyment, persuasion, and the exchange of information).

OBJECTIVES

Students will:

1. Explain Freud's theories of levels of consciousness, personality, stages of development, and defense mechanisms.
2. Use these theories to analyze fiction.
3. Analyze theme, imagery, foreshadowing, and character.
4. Use these literary elements in their writing.
5. Keep a journal or blog.
6. Create a PowerPoint or Keynote slide presentation.
7. Draw maps of the setting.
8. Create an original interpretation of the themes.
9. Support their views with text and outside references during discussion.
10. Conduct research.
11. Annotate the text.
12. Write one-paragraph essays.
13. Participate in discussions.

Lesson 1: Who Is Freud? Beginning the Novel

PROCEDURE

1. **Ask** students the following questions and discuss their answers:
   - What do you do when you come to the lunchroom and there are younger students ahead of you in line or sitting at a table that you would like to use?
   - Why not just make them move?
   - What might someone else do who was not as considerate? Why don't you do that?
   - Would it make a difference if there were no teachers there to supervise?

2. **Explain** the following:
   - In the early 1900s, a doctor named Sigmund Freud developed a theory about human personality that explains why we behave and feel the way we do. His theory would explain your responses to the previous questions.
   - He would say that you have developed certain personality traits that explain your behavior. This unit will examine his theories and use these explanations to analyze the events in the novel, *Lord of the Flies*.
   - His theories have been criticized as dated, but there isn't a current theory of personality that can't be traced back to the one developed by Freud. Criticizing him for being dated is like criticizing the Wright Brothers for not having a jet engine.
   - His theories also have been criticized as being sexist, but he wrote in Western Europe during the first half of the 20th century. These were sexist times and students will have to make their own judgments about the impact of the then-current views of women's roles on his theory.

3. **Discuss** the biography of Sigmund Freud's life that is found at the end of this chapter. (I do not have students take notes on this part of the lecture.)
4. **Ask** students how far back in their memory they can go. Have them recall their earliest memory and tell how old they were when the event occurred.
5. **Explain** that Freud said that our earliest experiences, particularly those related to family and safety, shape our personalities. Using the summary of Freud's theory that follows his biography at the end of this chapter, discuss the three aspects of personality: id, ego, and super-ego. Have students take notes.
6. **Explain** that the three main characters in *Lord of the Flies* exemplify these aspects of the personality, but that students will have to determine which character represents which aspect.

7. **Give** each student a copy of the grading sheet from the end of this chapter. Review each topic on the sheet. Explain that the point distribution is tentative and that it may change, depending on which aspects of the unit students choose to focus. For example, if discussion turns out to be a more important part of the unit than anticipated, the point value assigned to discussion will be increased. Also, it assumes that you will be giving the students a final, which is not included in this unit. You may adapt the grading sheet as you wish.

8. **Explain** that when students read passages for discussion, they will often use a technique called "Lord of the Flies Theatre." When students use this *reader's theatre* technique, you will assign a narrator to read all of the non-dialogue text, as well as roles for the characters who speak in the passages. Students should try to read in a way that captures the mood of the passages.

9. **Ask** students what *imagery* is. (The use of description that allows the reader to visualize the scene and the setting. It often creates a particular mood or feeling for the passages.)

10. **Have** students read the first paragraph silently, marking the phrases that help them visualize either the island or the boy. Students also should annotate phrases that the author used to create a consistent feeling (or mood) throughout the paragraph. Explain that the meaning of the scar will become clear in the first few pages and that creepers are long vines.

11. **Discuss** the paragraph:
    - What phrases did you note?
    - What feeling was the author trying to create? (e.g., humidity, heat)
    - Why might the author have chosen this mood for the opening of the book?
    - (He wanted to make the island seem tropical or jungle-like.)

12. **Assign** the parts of narrator, Ralph, and Piggy. Use the reader's theatre technique to read the rest of pages 1–3.

13. **Discuss** the passage:
    - What kind of imagery is used to describe Piggy? (Negative, almost pig-like)
    - What does Ralph's headstand say about his reaction to the crash? (He is not distressed.)
    - What is Ralph's response to Piggy? What is Piggy's response to Ralph? (Ralph seems to ignore Piggy, but Piggy follows Ralph.)
    - What happened to the plane and the passenger compartment? How was the scar formed? How does the description of the plane tell us that this plane doesn't really exist? (The passenger compartment of the plane was separated from the main body in the attack, cutting across the island. The storm that was occurring during the attack washed it into the ocean. This is how the scar was formed.) This is a difficult set

of questions. Students usually want to assume the time period is World War II (WWII). However, the facts that there is a passenger capsule that can separate from the cabin and, as we learn on page 9, England is under attack from an atomic bomb, indicate that Golding wanted the story to be timeless. This vagueness about the time period is discussed further below.

- Why doesn't Piggy run? (He has an ingrained concern with rules.)

14. **Have** students read the two paragraphs on top of page 5. Tell them to mark the passage for details that provide insight into Ralph's personality and physical appearance (or write this on a piece of paper if they are unable to write in their books).
    - What does the way in which he removes his clothes indicate about his personality? (He is impulsive or carefree.)
    - What phrases help you form an image of what Ralph looks like? What does this imagery seems to characterize Ralph as? (An angel or a statue of an angel.)

15. **Explain** that the phrase "proclaimed no devil" (p. 5) will become important in understanding an upcoming passage.

16. **Assign** the parts of narrator, Ralph, and Piggy. Use the reader's theatre technique to read page 8.

17. **Discuss** the passage:
    - How does Ralph react when he sees the pool? Which of Freud's personality aspects does this suggest? (He inspects the area and then plunges in. Ego, because before plunging in, he checks the area, thus suggesting a balance between impulse and safety.)
    - Contrast this with the way Piggy gets into the water. What aspect of the personality is suggested by Piggy's behavior? (He doesn't jump as Ralph does, but tiptoes carefully. He won't swim because he has internalized his aunt's rules. This seems to reflect the super-ego because he seems overly careful and driven by what rules tell him to do.)

HOMEWORK

Students should complete the following:

Finish reading Chapter 1. Annotate the chapter for imagery, labeling the overall effect of the imagery as positive or negative. Also annotate any actions that suggest aspects of Freud's theory of personality.

Lesson 2: Chapter 1

PROCEDURE

1. **Have** students orally summarize the events of Chapter 1.
2. **Have** students work in small groups to list characteristics of the three key aspects of Freud's personality theory. Have the groups share their lists and make a whole-group list. Be sure this list includes the following:

   - **Id**
     - Impulsive
     - Selfish/lack of concern with others
     - Animalistic
     - Immediate gratification
     - Lack of concern with consequences
     - Destructive in the extreme
     - Inborn
     - Guided by the pleasure principle

   - **Super-ego**
     - Moral standards/guided by morality principle
     - Long-term goals and consequences
     - Aware of conscience
     - Uses guilt or anxiety to achieve goals
     - Driven by rules and behavior that benefits the group
     - Internal voice of parents and society
     - Develops in young children

   - **Ego**
     - Your self-concept
     - Moderator between id and super-ego
     - Develops in infants
     - Governed by reality principle
     - Has defense mechanisms when reality is too difficult to deal with
     - Delays gratification

3. **Ask** students to speculate which of the three main characters represents each of the main aspects of Freud's personality theory. (Piggy correlates to super-ego, Jack correlates to id, and Ralph correlates to ego. Accept students' answers, even if they do not match up correctly. Students tend to understand what is represented in the characters in time.)
4. **Discuss** the following questions:

- On page 9, how does the reference to atom bomb reinforce the idea that the story's time period is intentionally vague and not WWII? (There was no atomic bombing of England during WWII.)
- On page 12, how does Piggy's plan to use the conch to organize a meeting and his refusal to blow it because of his aunt's rules reflect Freud's theory? (These events suggest super-ego because they are behaviors based on internalized rules and the good of the group.)

5. **Assign** the parts of narrator, Ralph, Jack, Sam, Eric, and Piggy. Use the reader's theatre technique to read from the choir's entrance on page 16 to where Ralph reveals Piggy's name on page 18.

6. **Discuss** the passage:
   - From the beginning of the passage to where Jack asks about a man being here, what words and phrases help you visualize Jack and the choir? (e.g., "something dark." Golding refers to the choir as "the creature"; "hidden by black cloaks"; "gasping, sweating, swaying in the fierce light" [p. 16].)
   - Compare the imagery Golding uses to describe Jack and the choir with that he uses to describe Ralph. (Ralph is described as an angel, while Jack is described as a devil.)
   - What happened to Simon and how did the others respond? How would Freud characterize this response? (He fainted from thirst. The others followed Jack's reaction, sniggered, and did nothing to help. Freud would say it is id-based behavior because it shows no concern for others.)
   - Why does Jack call Piggy "Fatty"? (He doesn't like the rules; Piggy is an easy target.)

7. **Have** students silently read the paragraph on the bottom of page 19 and the top of page 20 where the boys elect Ralph chief.

8. **Discuss** the paragraph:
   - What personality trait does each of the three main characters possess that would make him a good chief? (Piggy is intelligent; Jack is a natural leader; Ralph has a calmness about him.)
   - Why is Ralph elected chief? (He has the conch.)
   - What does the conch symbolize? (Accept students' answers—if they do not focus on organization and society at this point, they will soon enough.)

9. **Have** a student read aloud from the last paragraph on page 29 to the end of the chapter.

10. **Discuss** the passage:

- Summarize the events that began when the boys came upon the piglet and end when the boys move down the scar to the meeting. (A group of boys are hunting in the forest, and they come upon a piglet. Jack starts to stab it, but can't bring himself to do so. He then makes excuses for not killing it.)
- Why does Jack say he didn't kill the piglet? (He claims that he was looking for the right place to stick the knife.)
- What does Golding suggest is Jack's reason for not killing the piglet? (It was an "enormous" decision that Jack wasn't ready to make. That is why he hesitated and why his face turned pale.)
- What would Freud say was the reason for Jack's hesitation? (Because he had internalized society's rule that killing is bad. He was limited by his super-ego.)

HOMEWORK

Students should complete the following:

Review Chapter 1. Draw a map of the island that includes all of the places Golding details; label each landmark. Do not color the map because you will be adding more details as you read further. Read Chapter 2, annotating or denoting any examples or symbols of order and chaos.

Lesson 3: Chapter 2

PROCEDURE

1. **Have** students work in partners and present their maps to each other. Students should add details to their own maps that they had omitted but that their partner had included. Explain that students should continue adding landmarks to the maps as they read about new places on the island. The maps will be collected and graded at the end of the unit.

2. **Have** students orally summarize Chapter 2.

3. **Ask** students to summarize a few specific passages from the chapter that they think are particularly representative of id, ego, and super-ego. Allow other students to agree with or dispute the proffered connections between the suggested passages and personality aspect.

4. **Assign** the roles of narrator, Ralph, and the two unidentified boys. Use the reader's theatre technique to read the passage on page 32 beginning with "the meeting hummed" and ending on page 33 with Jack saying what will happen if anyone breaks the rules.

5. **Discuss** the passage:
   - What is the conch used for? (Maintaining order when boys want to speak.)
   - What aspect of the personality does the conch represent? Why? (Super-ego, because it is a symbol for rules.)
   - What is Jack's attitude toward rules? How would Freud explain Jack feeling this way? (Jack likes rules. He appears either to have a strong super-ego or a very repressed id.)

6. **Assign** the roles of narrator, Piggy, Ralph, and Jack. Use the reader's theatre technique to read the passage beginning on page 35 when the small boy holds out his hand and ends on page 37 when Ralph says they want to have fun and be rescued.

7. **Discuss** the passage:
   - What is the little boy afraid of? (A beastie.)
   - How do the rest of the boys respond to his concern? How do Ralph and Jack respond? (The boys become restless when the little boy talks about it. The littluns seem to take the claim seriously. Ralph gives logical reasons why there couldn't be a beastie or snake on the island. Jack supports Ralph, but still offers plan for hunting it down.)
   - Why is Ralph annoyed with Jack's response? (Because Jack gives some support for the idea that Ralph says is impossible and this undermines Ralph.)
   - Is there a beast on the island? (Accept and discuss all answers. Explain that the group will explore this question again later.)

- What aspect of Freud's personality theory is revealed in Ralph's plan to have fun and be rescued? (Ego, because it represents a balance between the need to have fun that is suggestive of the id and the long-term goal for the good of the group that is suggestive of the super-ego.)

8. **Discuss** the rest of the chapter:
   - How does the fire represent both super-ego and id? (Super-ego: When controlled, it represents a long-term goal for the good of group/society. Id: When it gets out of control and the boys don't think of the consequences, it becomes destructive.)
   - How would Freud explain Piggy's role in the remainder of the chapter? (Piggy is the super-ego of the group. He criticizes them for not planning well—not taking names, not building shelters. He reminds them of the consequences of bad behavior: The littlun died in the fire; the firewood was burned up; they almost burned up the island.)
   - Who is responsible for the death of the boy in the fire? (Discuss all answers; however, students will probably focus on it having been an unfortunate accident.)

9. **Have** students silently read the first two paragraphs of Chapter 3 on page 50. Tell them to pay particular attention to the imagery and to how the totality of the imagery creates a particular mood.

10. **Discuss** the passage:
    - What phrases help you visualize Jack as he is hunting? (e.g., his nose is only inches from the humid Earth, he lowered his chin)
    - If you didn't know he was describing a boy, what might you think Golding is describing in this passage? (An animal hunting.)

HOMEWORK

You will need to decide if students are going to type or handwrite a journal or keep a blog. In either case, the guidelines and outcomes will be the same. The only difference that I have found, and I have conducted it both ways, is that students seem more enthusiastic about the blog. Should you have students use blogs, and you have the option, create them in-house on your school's server. Otherwise, there are several free blog sites on the web. I have used http://www.kidblog.org and http://edublogs.org, although the latter can at times be undependable, depending on the technology that you use.

When I taught this unit to my entire class, journal assignments were shorter, due to time needed for grading. Now I teach it to groups ranging in size from 4 to 12, and I use the following guidelines.

> **General Guidelines for Journals/Blogs**
>
> 1. Each entry should be approximately 2 pages, size 12 font, double spaced.
> 2. Do not change events from the book (e.g., your character must be male, cannot be over 12 years old, cannot have been going to America).
> 3. Do not use current vernacular without justification (e.g., "I was going to chill" or "BTW").
> 4. Entries should read as if Golding had written them.

Students should complete the following:

Create a journal/blog as one of nameless characters on the island. Write four or five entries corresponding to different turning points in the book. In addition, you will respond as your character to each other's journals.

Read the Excerpt From Journal/Blog Entry 1 that is included at the end of this chapter. Write the first entry using the following guidelines.

Guidelines for Journal/Blog Entry 1: Introducing Your Character and the First Meeting

1. Character (decide if your character is essentially driven by id, ego, or super-ego. This driving quality should be evident in the entry.)
   a. Include a physical description/body type (work it into a story).
   b. Describe the family background.
   c. Include an anecdote that reveals the kind of relationship that you had with one or more of your parents.
2. The island
   a. Through imagery that creates a mood (e.g., happy, scary), describe the island.
   b. Tell what you were doing when you heard the conch.
3. The meeting
   a. Describe your character's behavior at the meeting.
   b. Tell how your character reacts to the events he observes at the meeting.
   c. Tell for whom your character voted and why.

Lesson 4: More on Freud

PROCEDURE

1. **Have** a few students read aloud a segment of their journals/blogs. Other students should comment on the aspects of Freud's theory that were evident in the reading.

2. **Explain** that Freud's theory is much broader than his model of the personality and levels of consciousness. Besides these aspects of his theory, many other aspects also relate to the events and characters in the book. Students are to review the following websites (or other material you may have on hand) and write two- to three-sentence definitions for each of the following terms:

   - manifest content in dreams
   - latent content in dreams
   - ego defense mechanisms
   - rationalization
   - latency period as a stage of sexual development
   - anxiety
   - instinct

3. **Explain** that students may share research, work in partners, or divvy up the research; but they must each write their own definitions. Students are to review at least four different websites from the list. At the end of the definitions, students are to write a one-paragraph summary of one new Freudian concept about which they have read that will become the topic of a PowerPoint (or Keynote) presentation.

I tell students that they may not do a presentation on either the Oedipal complex or the Electra complex because they are too complicated and tangential to the book. I also tell them that they should keep their topic very specific—for example, one or two defense mechanisms, not all of them, or the concept in general.

Our school librarian, Linda Polack, has made a Filamentality Hotlinks list of these websites for students. You can reach this list by going to http://www.sunsetridge29.net, clicking on Sunset Ridge School at the top of the page, and then clicking on learning center in the drop-down menu. Click on Class Links on the left side; the Hotlist will appear as "Sigmund Freud Hotlist." In addition, the websites are listed below.

OVERVIEWS OF FREUD'S THEORY

- **Freud Museum London** (http://www.freud.org.uk): Includes biographical information and a photo library

- **Freud's Theories** (http://www.changingminds.org/explanations/behaviors/freud.htm): Includes theories on personality factors, defense mechanisms, transference, and psychosexual stage
- **Sigmund Freud (1856–1939), Internet Encyclopedia of Philosophy** (http://www.iep.utm.edu/freud): Offers detailed explanations of several concepts
- **Sigmund Freud Life and Work Theories** (http://www.freudfile.org/theory.html): Lists various Freud theories, with age-appropriate definitions

DREAM THEORY

- **Dream Theory According to Freud** (http://www.dreamlynx.com/thefreud.html): Offers an age-appropriate outline of related concepts
- **Introduction to Sigmund Freud's Theory on Dreams** (http://www.insomnium.co.uk/text/freud.htm): Provides an overview of Freud's dream theory

PERSONALITY THEORY

- **Sigmund Freud Personality Theories** (http://webspace.ship.edu/cgboer/freud.html): Provides a good overview of Freud's theories

TRANSFERENCE AND TRAUMA

- **Modules on Freud: On Transference and Trauma** (www.cla.purdue.edu/academic/engl/theory/psychoanalysis/freud5mainframe.html): Discusses transference and trauma

HOMEWORK

Students should complete the following:

After reading the sample journal/blog response, exchange journals or blog addresses. You should write, in character, a well-developed, one-paragraph response to the entry. For example, if you feel that your character could be a friend with the writer's character, the response could explain the basis for that friendship.

Read and annotate Chapter 3.

Lesson 5: Chapter 3

PROCEDURE

1. **Have** students orally summarize Chapter 3.
2. **Ask** a few students to share and discuss their responses to another character's first journal entry.
3. **Have** students share their definitions of the terms from the homework. Ask if they have come across any examples of the terms in the book. (Collect and grade, if you wish.)
4. **Explain** that students are to make a PowerPoint (or Keynote) presentation on a concept of Freud's that is related to the book, but that you did not review in detail at the beginning of the unit. It is to contain 5 or 6 slides and be no longer than 5 minutes. Students are to use the slides to highlight their main points, not to show all of their content. It will be graded 40% on presentation and 60% on content. (If your groups are large, let students work with partners and modify the requirements accordingly.)
5. **Distribute** the following guidelines:
   - Slide 1: Title card
     - Catchy title (I like requiring students to include a colon, e.g., Regression: Back to the Past)
     - Student name
     - Date

   - Slide 2: Detail one aspect of Freud's theory.
   - Slides 3–4: Give two examples from the book that illustrate the aspect.
   - Slide 5: Bibliography—Use at least two sources.

6. **Explain** that the presentation will not be due for a week to give students time to find the examples as they are completing their reading assignments. (I have a few students present each day, rather than have all of the presentations on the same day.)
7. **Have** students orally summarize a few specific passages from the chapter that they think are particularly representative of id, ego, and super-ego. Allow other students to agree with or dispute the proffered connections between the suggested passages and personality aspect.
8. **Assign** the roles of narrator, Simon, Jack, and Ralph. Use the reader's theater technique to read the passage that begins on the bottom of page 52 when the leaves come apart and ends on page 53 when Ralph complains that everyone is off bathing, or eating, or playing.
9. **Discuss** the passage:

- How successful is the building of the shelters? (They have built two shelters that are falling apart. Most of the boys are not working on them anymore.)
- Why do they need the shelters? (In case storms come and to protect them from the beastie.)
- What aspect of Freud's personality theory do the shelters represent? Why? (Super-ego, because they represent a long-term goal that is for the good of the community.)

10. **Discuss** the paragraph on page 56 when Jack describes how he feels when he is hunting in the jungle:
- How does Jack feel when he is in the jungle? (He feels as if he is being hunted.)
- How would Freud explain this feeling? (The jungle is uncivilized, and Jack is unprotected from his id. This is particularly evident in the jungle because here Jack does not have the surroundings of civilization that are needed to reinforce his super-ego or to bolster his ego's attempts to limit his id.)

11. **Discuss** the passage that begins on page 59 and continues to the end of the chapter.
- What has been Simon's role thus far? Give some examples of Simon's behavior. (He has been kind. He has been a helper. He defended Piggy when Jack said Piggy did not help with the fire [page 43]. He was one of the only boys to build the shelter [page 52]. He picked fruit for the littluns—[page 59].)
- What phrases does Golding use to create an image of Simon's hiding place in the jungle on pages 60–61? What mood do these phrases create? ("sunshine fell," "aromatic bushes," "gaudy butterflies that danced," "fantastic birds," and "flowers rose delicately to meet the open air." The mood is positive and beautiful. The spot is a sanctuary.)
- Why does Jack feel he is being hunted when he is alone in the jungle, but Simon feels safe when he is alone in the same location? (Jack is driven more by id. When he is alone, he confronts his true nature. Simon is kind, so when he is alone and confronts his true nature, he isn't threatened by something bad. He is good and sees the jungle as good; Jack is driven by id and sees the jungle as dangerous because id uncontrolled is dangerous.)
- How does Simon fit into Freud's model? (Simon does not seem to exhibit signs of id, so he does not seem to need an ego to balance the id. Thus, he seems to fall outside the model.)
- Simon has been compared to an angel. Do you agree? (Discuss different answers. He seems to exist outside the model to represent pure

goodness, like an angel. He shows the potential of a person without id-driven impulses.)

HOMEWORK

Students should complete the following:

Read the Excerpt From Journal/Blog Entry 2 that is included at the end of this chapter. Write the second entry using the following guidelines:

Guidelines for Journal/Blog Entry 2: Your Reaction to the Jungle

1. The jungle as metaphor
   a. Tell where you were and what you were doing when Jack was hunting alone (e.g., hunting, building huts).
      i. If your character's strongest personality is id (as is the case with most people), use imagery to create a scary mood as you describe the activity.
      ii. If your character's strongest aspect is super-ego, the jungle may seem a place for order or safety.
      iii. Start your character outside the jungle and bring him inside.
         1. Perhaps start describing your reaction to building huts.
         2. Perhaps describe the beach as a place of safety—as a contrast to the jungle.

Read and annotate Chapter 4.

Lesson 6: Chapter 4

PROCEDURE

1. **Have** a few students read a segment of their journals/blogs. Other students should comment on the aspects of Freud's theory that were evident in the reading.

At this point in the unit, I often assign students chapters for which they are to lead the discussion. When this happens, I show them the passages I would highlight for discussion, and then have them make notes on possible answers. The students then lead the discussions instead of me, using either the passages I recommended or others that they feel are significant to moving the story forward. Chapter 4 has several short, but poignant, passages that work well for student-led discussions. Several of them are pointed out below.

2. **Have** students orally summarize Chapter 4.

3. **Have** students summarize a few specific passages from the chapter that they think are particularly representative of id, ego, and super-ego. Allow other students to agree with or dispute the proffered connections between the suggested passages and the personality aspect.

4. **Ask** which characters represent the three main aspects of Freud's personality theory. Ask if they have changed their answers since you first asked this question.

5. **Discuss** the passage on page 64 that begins with the three boys playing and ends on page 65 with Maurice trotting off:
   • What do Roger and Maurice do to the littluns? What is each one's responsibility in the destruction? (Roger leads the destruction of the sandcastle, and then Maurice adds to the damage.)
   • How does Maurice feel afterward? How would Freud explain both his action and his reaction? (Freud would explain Maurice's action as id-driven because Maurice is destroying the boys' castle to have fun. The guilt he feels afterward is the internal voice of parents, or the super-ego. The guilt doesn't last, however.)

6. **Discuss** the passage that begins on the bottom of page 66 with the description of the subsoil and ends on page 67 with the key statement that civilization is in ruins:
   • How would Freud explain Roger intentionally throwing the stones to miss Henry? (Freud would say that this cruel behavior is founded in Roger's id because Roger is engaging in it purely for fun. Although this behavior is not prevented by the super-ego, it is restricted. "Taboos" and "laws" refer to rules that have been internalized.)

- Why is it important to the story that Golding tells us the civilization from which the boys had come is in ruins? (It tells us that the violence we have seen thus far is not simply because the boys lack adult supervision. It is because violence is inherent in people. The adults have destroyed civilization and have thus committed violent acts against each other.)
- What is foreshadowing? What might this event foreshadow? (It is the suggestion of a future event in the piece. This event might suggest that Roger will destroy something with rocks.)

7. **Have** students meet in three small groups. Assign each group one of the following three topics to prepare for discussion with the entire class. Then have each group take turns leading a class discussion on its assigned topic.

While groups are meeting, I go around and have brief conferences with each student to review and grade the annotations in his or her book.

GROUP 1: THE MASKS
- Why does Jack say he paints his face? (So the pigs won't see him when he hunts.)
- How does painting his face change Jack's behavior and his personality? (Jack so likes his awesome image that he begins to dance. The mask frees him from shame.)
- Why does Golding have Jack compare the paint to the military? (Because what the boys do on the island is similar to what adults do in the real world.)
- How would Freud explain the mask? (The mask liberates the id from shame and shame is what the super-ego uses to control the id.)

GROUP 2: THE HUNT
- How does the mask make this attempt to kill the pig more successful than the last attempt? (Without shame, they can ignore society's rule against killing.)
- Why would Freud say they hunt instead of attending to the fire? (The mask frees the boys' id and thus the immediate impulse to hunt and eat is consuming. The fire is a long-term, communal goal, suggestive of super-ego and they are free from super-ego-based concerns.)
- Make a case for the belief that Jack does not want to go home. (Jack likes being free from society's constraints and thus does not want a ship to rescue them. Golding says hunting was fierce exhilaration for Jack but the outside world was baffled commonsense. Jack prefers the former.)

A Freudian Analysis of Literature   **67**

GROUP 3: THE CONFLICT

- How would Freud explain Jack's lack of concern for the huts and fire? How would Freud explain Jack's focus on hunting? (Huts and the fire are part of the "baffling commonsense"—of the long-term goal related to what is best for the group. Jack is concerned with what is best for him right now.)

- Why does Jack hit Piggy? (The mask frees him from super-ego so he can be violent without fear of either consequences or the shame associated with breaking society's rules. Golding suggests that Jack is humiliated because Ralph has criticized him. Because of the mask he is finally "able at last to hit someone" [p. 77] so he transfers his anger to Piggy who is a more acceptable target.)

- Why should Jack care about breaking Piggy's specs? Why doesn't he? (They will need them later, but long-term concerns are based in the super-ego and Jack is liberated from this.)

- Why, at the end of the chapter (p. 82), is Ralph both envious and resentful of the hunters? (Because he wants to participate in the fun but knows other things are more important to the rescue effort. He resents the fact that the other boys can have the fun he can't.)

HOMEWORK

Students should complete the following:

Begin preparing for the mandatory/optional project. You will present a creative interpretation of the book's and Freud's themes at the end of the unit. This project must be founded on the events in the book, but it also must extend the themes revealed in these events. It cannot simply be a retelling of the content in another way. Therefore, a comic book of one of the chapters would not work, but a dance that shows how the three boys would respond to the influences of id, ego, and super-ego could be acceptable.

Complete the following sentences in preparation for the homework:

- Someone who is too driven by id is _____. (overly impulsive, selfish)
- Someone who is too driven by ego is _____. (overly analytical)
- Someone who is too driven by super-ego is _____. (overly inhibited, a follower)

Write a one-paragraph summary of your (or your group's) project and a one-paragraph explanation of how this project extends the themes of the book and Freud. You will only need one write-up for each group if you are doing a group project.

Exchange journals with someone other than the person with whom you exchanged previously. Write a one-paragraph response to something in the second entry. In the response, students should display behavior or attitudes that show which of the three personality aspects drives their character. Read the Sample Response to a Journal Blog Entry at the end of this chapter.

Read and annotate Chapter 5.

I let students work alone or in groups as large as four members. They come to school at night for "The Feast," where we order ribs and present the projects. This allows students from different sections of the class to work together on the group projects. We eat and then evaluate the presentations together. This, of course, is not necessary for the completion of the unit; adjust the presentation requirements and schedule to meet your needs.

Here is a list of some successful projects that you might want to share with your class:

- Closing statements from the prosecution and defense attorneys at Jack's trial for the murder of Piggy.
- Ralph's and Jack's speeches at Piggy's memorial.
- Models of Ralph's, Jack's, and Piggy's bedrooms, reflecting their personalities.
- "Where Are They Now?" showing several characters as adults.
- Jack's Travel Agency for vacations on the island, complete with brochures and a commercial.
- Rewriting the final part of the book as Act 5 of a Shakespearean tragedy.

Lesson 7: Chapter 5—The Essential Illness

PROCEDURE

1. **Have** some students read their responses to the second journal entry. Other students should discuss which personality trait was most evident in the reading.

2. **Have** students read aloud the paragraph summaries of their projects. Approve them or make suggestions for improvement. The criteria for approval should include the following:
   - Does the project blend at least one key theme of the novel with one major aspect of Freud's theory?
   - Does the project use these to support a topic that extends a significant part of the novel?
   - Is the project expansive enough to justify the time allotted?

I once had a project proposal that suggested Jack and Ralph each present a set of rules by which the boys should live. Although this met the first two guidelines, it did not meet the third one. I therefore suggested that the project include not only the rules, but also a campaign that each boy would present. This included speeches, a campaign slogan, posters, and an introduction presented by another character serving as a campaign manager.

3. **Have** a student orally summarize Chapter 5.

4. **Have** students summarize a few specific passages from the chapter that they think are particularly representative of id, ego, and super-ego. Allow other students to agree with or dispute the proffered connections between the suggested passages and personality aspect.

5. **Have** students review at least three of the following pages: 1, 5, 8, 16, 31, 50, and 84, to discern a pattern of the reoccurring symbolism of clothing. They should discuss or write about what clothing symbolizes and how the symbol changes as the boys spend more time on the island. (Clothing reflects the boys' attitude toward civilization or super-ego. Ralph, for example, is carefree about his clothing when he first goes in the water, but Piggy carefully folds his. This suggests that Ralph is lax about rules, but Piggy is fastidious about them. As the boys spend more time on the island, their clothing gets more tattered—as do the rules of society.)

6. **Check** students' maps to be sure they include the details of the meeting place from the middle of page 84 to the top of page 85.

7. **Have** students work in small groups to list the rules that Ralph chastises the boys for breaking.
   - People drink from the river.
   - People aren't building the huts.
   - People aren't going to the lavatory in the rocks.

- People aren't keeping the fire going.
- The fire got out of control.

8. **Discuss** the meeting (page 86 to the end of the chapter):
   - How do the boys respond to Ralph's criticism? (They snigger and complain that he has too many rules.)
   - What points does Jack make at the meeting? (Jack turns the discussion to fear. He denies the existence of the beast, but at the same time, suggests that he would hunt it.)
   - Where do the boys think the beast lives? Why is the location significant? (After Ralph argues that there is no beast in the jungle, the littluns suggest it lives in the sea [p. 97]—thus surrounding them.)
   - What does Simon suggest the beast is? Why isn't Simon afraid of the jungle at night when the rest of the boys are? (The rest of the boys fear the beast may be in the jungle. Therefore, the jungle represents or holds their fears. Simon does not fear the beast as a creature in the jungle. Rather, he suggests that the beast is a manifestation of the boys themselves. Therefore, when he is in the jungle, he is away from the boys and away from what he understands to be the beast.)
   - Golding states that Simon is inarticulate in expressing "mankind's essential illness" (p. 98). What would Golding and Freud say this illness is? (Stress that this is the essential question of the book. Golding suggests that there is an evil quality to human nature that leads to destruction. The outside world is at war and the boys' society is breaking down. That is why Golding says that the lawful world is slipping away. Freud would explain this as id out of control, unrestrained by internalized laws and rules.)
   - How would Golding and Freud explain Jack saying, "Bollocks to the rules!" (p. 101)? How would they explain the meeting breaking up? (Golding would explain this as Jack wanting the lawful world to slip away. Freud would say that Jack is driven by his id—therefore, he prefers hunting and does not like rules that are founded in the super-ego. The meeting breaks up because the super-ego—symbolized by the conch—isn't strong enough to suppress the id. Golding would say this breakup reveals mankind's illness—the inability to behave in a civilized manner.)

9. **Ask**, "Why does Ralph want a sign from the grown-up world?" (He thinks grown-ups would be civilized [i.e., keep the fire going, not quarrel]. A sign from them might encourage the boys to behave in the same manner.)

HOMEWORK
Students should complete the following:

Read and annotate Chapters 6 and 7. Continue to work on the final project.

Lesson 8: Chapters 6 and 7—The Turning Point?

PROCEDURE

1. **Have** students orally summarize Chapters 6 and 7.
2. **Ask** students to summarize a few specific passages from the chapter that they think are particularly representative of id, ego, and super-ego. Allow other students to agree with or dispute the proffered connections between the suggested passages and personality aspect.
3. **Create** a plot graph. Draw a large *x* and *y* axis for a graph on a whiteboard. Draw a large X inside the graph and circle the point at which the lines intersect.

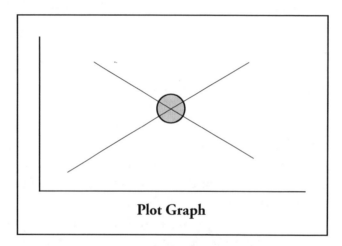

Plot Graph

4. **Ask** students to explain how the "X" in the graph represents the plot of the book. Students may need to break into small groups to discuss this question, but I have never had a group that couldn't see the line that drops from left to right as super-ego on the island and the line that rises from right to left as id. Ask students if the story has reached the point at which the lines have crossed. (Accept and discuss all answers.)
5. **Discuss** the dead paratrooper landing on the island (pp. 106–107):
   • How did the paratrooper end up on the island? (There was an air battle above the island. His plane was shot and he died in the attack.)
   • What is dramatic irony? (An outcome or event that is contrary to what was, or might have been, expected.)
   • Why is the paratrooper's body landing on the island ironic? (Because Ralph wanted a sign from the adult world to bring civilization to the island. He got the sign, but instead of it representing civilization, it represents war and destruction.)

- How does the body move? (When the breeze blows, it catches the parachute and lifts the body up. When the wind dies down, the body falls forward, again.)

6. **Assign** the parts of narrator, Sam, Eric, Ralph, and Jack. Use the reader's theatre technique to read the passage that begins on page 111 with, "They lay there listening" and ends on page 114 when Jack disregards the conch.

7. **Discuss** the passage:
   - What is the mood that Golding creates in the beginning of the passage? How does Golding use imagery to establish this mood? (The mood is one of fear and menace. He creates this mood through the use of dark images such as the following: darkness was full of claws, stars faded out, and sad and grey light filtering into the shelters.)
   - How do Jack and Ralph react to Sam and Eric's report? How would Freud characterize these reactions? (Jack immediately wants to hunt the beast. He has no concerns for the littluns, further suggesting id's disregard for the needs of the group. This is an impulsive id-based reaction because it is immediate and not thought out. Ralph, in contrast, thinks through the hunt, thus suggesting ego weighing the pros and cons of going after the beast. He questions the use of wood spears and shows concern for the littluns.)
   - Why would Freud say Jack disregards the conch? (The conch symbolizes order and society, and Jack wants decisions based on his own id-centered, selfish behavior.)

8. **Have** students compare and contrast Jack's and Ralph's reactions to the newly explored section of the island at the end of the chapter. (Ralph calls it a "rotten place" [p. 119] and thinks ahead about the realities of living in this setting without water—a long-term goal centered in the super-ego. He comments about the lack of water. Jack, in contrast, is only concerned about the location as a fort—suggestive of battle and destruction.)

9. **Explain** that Jack's plan to crush an enemy with the rock (p. 120) is foreshadowing. Ask what event this might predict.

10. **Have** a student read aloud the second paragraph on page 124 in which Ralph reflects on the boys' appearance.

11. **Discuss** the passage:
    - What phrases does Golding use to help the reader visualize the boys? What mood does this imagery create? (Phrases such as "Hair much too long, tangled here and there . . . clothes, worn away" [p. 124] suggest a depressed mood and create an image of society being further worn away.)
    - How does this image of the boys' appearance compare to the pattern of their declining appearance discussed a few days ago? (Their appearance

continues to deteriorate. Their clothing is in a more advanced stage of ruin, suggesting that civilization is similarly in a more advanced stage of decay.)

- When this description of clothing is added to the ones reviewed earlier, how does the reoccurring image of clothing compare to the descending super-ego line on the plot grid? (Guide students to articulate that in the beginning, clothing was clean and emblematic of society. At that point super-ego was high. Both continue to deteriorate as id becomes stronger.)

12. **Have** students contrast Ralph's daydream on the bottom of page 126 and the top of page 127 of life in England with life on the island. Ask why Golding presents this contrasting image. (In Ralph's daydream, England is cold and the snow covers the ground with a clean layer of white. The island, in contrast, is hot and the jungle is dark. The wild animals in England are peaceful ponies. On the island, the wild animals are untamed pigs. In England, Ralph is surrounded with symbols of society such as books and bowls of corn flakes. On the island, he eats grey fruit and hunts for pigs. In short, in England, "Everything was all right" [p. 127]. This highlights the fact that on the island, in contrast, everything connected to civilization is breaking down.)

13. **Point out** that this daydream marks a turning point on the island and that events are about to become worse.

14. **Assign** the parts of narrator, Maurice, Ralph, Jack, and Robert. Have everyone read the boys' chanting. Use the reader's theatre technique to read the passage that begins on page 128 with Ralph saying that he hit the pig and ends on 130 when Ralph's desire to hurt was overwhelming.

15. **Discuss** the passage:
   - How does Ralph feel about having wounded the boar? (He is proud of himself. This pride is seen when he suns himself in the respect of the hunters.)
   - How does Jack respond to Ralph wounding the boar? (He devalues Ralph's efforts and heightens his role in wounding the boar. He says he walloped him, and that Ralph should have waited.)
   - Describe the role-play in which the boys use Robert to recreate the attack on the boar. What is Ralph's reaction to the "game"? (The game gets out of hand and Robert gets hurt. Ralph becomes caught up in hurting Robert, but also is "frightened" by his desire to hurt the boy.)
   - How would Freud characterize Ralph's participation and reaction? (Ralph is caught up in the moment and is not at first concerned about the consequences of Robert getting hurt. Then he feels guilty about this reaction and stops himself from going further. This suggests an action founded in the id that is limited by the super-ego.)

16. **Ask**, "On page 134, Ralph asks Jack, 'Why do you hate me?' Jack does not answer. What would Freud say is the reason for Jack's feelings?" (Jack is driven by his id, whereas Ralph has an ego that considers id's desires, but tempers it with super-ego-based constraints. Jack does not want to be constrained.)

17. **Ask**, "When the boys come across the dead paratrooper, why do they run?" (When they confront what they think is really the beast, they follow their impulse to flee. This is in contrast to their imagined reaction to hunt the beast. The supposed reality is too frightening to confront.)

HOMEWORK

Students should complete the following:

Read and annotate Chapter 8, and continue working on the final project. In this chapter, both Golding's themes and Freud's theory are explicitly stated so annotate in detail.

Lesson 9: Chapter 8—Small Group Work

PROCEDURE

1. **Let** students begin to read Chapter 9 while you take their books (or notes, if they have been unable to write on their books) one at a time and grade their annotations.

2. **Have** a student orally summarize Chapter 8.

3. **Ask** students to summarize a few specific passages from the chapter that they think are particularly representative of id, ego, and super-ego. Allow other students to agree with or dispute the proffered connections between the suggested passages and personality aspect.

4. **Divide** the students into six groups and have each group prepare a discussion of one of the following six passages. Give them the following questions as a guide for their preparation. Tell students to address the book's themes and Freud's view whenever appropriate.

GROUP 1: FROM THE BEGINNING OF PAGE 142 TO PAGE 145 WHEN JACK GOES OFF BY HIMSELF

- What is Ralph's view of hunting the beast? (Ralph seems to have weighed the pros and cons, which suggests strong ego. He has come to the realistic conclusion that they wouldn't really hunt the beast because it is too big. This explains why the boys ran away after confronting the paratrooper.)

- How does Jack respond to Ralph's view? Why? (Jack's self-concept of himself as the big hunter cannot accept that he would be flawed. He therefore blames and devalues Ralph, calling him a coward and not a hunter to cover up his own insecurity about being seen as someone who would run away.)

- Discuss the irony in Jack's statement that the beast is a hunter. (Jack doesn't realize that the truth in his statement refers to himself and his id-driven personality.)

- Why are the boys feeling shame for their vote? (They feel guilty for their real feelings of wanting Jack—which is why they sneak off after him.)

GROUP 2: FROM THE BOTTOM OF PAGE 151 WHEN JACK IS STANDING IN FRONT OF THE GROUP TO PAGE 152 WHEN JACK SUGGESTS THAT LEAVING A TRIBUTE MIGHT KEEP THE BEAST FROM BOTHERING THEM

- Why does Golding remind us that the boys once had an angelic quality? (This is in contrast to the reference to the boys as hunters that is in the next sentence. Freud would say this is a reminder of their once sublimated drives into socially acceptable ways that now come out in savage hunting.)

- What is the meaning of Jack's instructions to leave something for the beast? (This further heightens their descent into savagery or their further loss of super-ego. It suggests savage or pagan worship of the evilness.)
- Why is it thoughtless to kill the female pig? (Because it cannot nurture the piglets that might have grown up to supply the food that they will need in the long term. But being driven by id, they do not think of long-term consequences to their behavior.)
- Contrast this killing to the attack of the boar. (This is much easier and less threatening as the female does not fight back. Thus, Jack runs little risk of being hurt this time.)

GROUP 3: FROM THE BEGINNING OF PAGE 156 TO THE BOTTOM OF THE PAGE WHEN THE BOYS RUN AWAY

- Why do the boys sharpen the stick at both ends? (To mount the head of the pig as a sacrifice to the beast. It suggests a pagan ritual and highlights their decent into savagery.)
- Why do the boys draw back at the sight of the pig's head on the stick? (This is an instinctual or id-based reaction to the horror of the sight. It is the first time that the boys see flies attracted to their deed.)
- Why do the boys run away? (This is also an instinctual or id-based reaction to the horror of the sight.)

GROUP 4: ALL OF PAGE 160

- What kind of imagery does Golding use to describe Jack and the group that steals the fire? Why does he choose this particular image? (He describes them as demons—painted faces, howling. This highlights how savage these boys have become.)
- Why is it significant that Jack is naked during the attack? (Clothing is a symbol of civilization. The boys' clothing has continually been getting more and more ruined as civilization breaks down. Now that the boys have stolen what they could have asked for and received, they have descended so far into savagery that they have no need for the symbol of civilization.)
- How would Freud characterize Jack's invitation to the feast? (It is the essence of id. Jack offers hunting, feasting, and fun, all of which are immediate and pleasurable and have nothing to do with concerns for a rescue. The invitation is also centered on Jack giving permission. This again shows Jack's lack of concern for the group and suggests that in his group, there will be no group process.)
- How would Freud characterize Jack having painted his face and destroying the fire? (The mask, as Golding points out, frees Jack from shame. This again highlights his loss of super-ego, which uses shame and guilt to contain the id. The fire is the boys' plan for rescue. Jack has no concern for this long-term, super-ego-based plan or for what the group needs.)

GROUP 5: FROM THE MIDDLE OF PAGE 163 WHEN THE LORD OF THE FLIES SPEAKS TO SIMON TO THE END OF THE CHAPTER

- Is Simon actually having a conversation with the beast? (Golding is vague about what is happening, but he suggests that Simon is epileptic—fainting, swollen tongue, head tilted back. But this may be a pathway to his clarity or he may be hallucinating.)
- What does the beast say he is? Why can't they hunt the beast? (The head confirms Simon's earlier proposition that the beast is a part of them. They can't hunt it because, being a part of them, it will be wherever they are.)
- What would both Golding and Freud say is the significance of the beast saying that he is the reason it's "no go" (p. 164) and that "we are going to have fun" (p. 164)? (Golding is alluding to mankind's essential illness—his destructive nature. Jack has just destroyed the fire and, exactly like the beast, has just said staying on the island would be fun. Freud would attribute Jack's behavior to the inevitable triumph of id over super-ego and id's focus on pleasurable things with no sense of consequences.)

5. **Discuss** the following questions:
   - The title of the book can be traced back to a translation form ancient Hebrew and Greek and is often used as a reference to Satan. Why did Golding choose this for the title? (He suggests that the evil in human nature is connected to satanic evil—an evil so powerful, it triumphs over humankind's good instincts. Ultimately this evil is what people worship because it is what is at the core of human personality. Therefore, people worship the evil in human nature.)
   - Where would you place the plot at the end of the chapter on the "X" diagram? Why? (Accept and discuss several answers.)

HOMEWORK

Students should complete the following:

Read the Excerpt From Journal/Blog Entry 3 that is included at the end of this chapter. Write the third journal entry using the following guidelines:

Guidelines for Journal/Blog Entry 3: Choosing Sides

1. Whose side are you on?
   a. Discuss your decision to join Jack's tribe or to remain with Ralph.
   b. Did you do what you wanted or what you thought was the right thing to do?
   c. Were you pressured into your decision?

d. Why did you make the decision you did?
2. Include references to the other group.
    a. Do you despise them? Fear them?
    b. Do you want them back?
    c. Do you think they are stupid or selfish?
3. Discuss your new life in the group.
    a. Use imagery to do this.
    b. Describe the setting and events.

Read and annotate Chapter 9.

Lesson 10: Chapter 9—Thesis Statements

PROCEDURE

1. **Have** students summarize a few specific passages from the chapter that they think are particularly representative of Freud's theory. Allow other students to agree with or dispute the proffered connections between the suggested passages and personality aspect.

2. **Ask** a few students to read aloud and explicate an excerpt from their character's third journal entry. Explain that they will not be responding to each other's third entries for homework because there will be another entry tonight for this chapter.

3. **Ask** where students think the story is on the plot graph at the end of this chapter.
   - Has id surpassed super-ego?
   - At what moment in the story did this happen?

4. **Explain** that beginning with this chapter, students will start preparing for the final examination. The final exam included at the end of this chapter consists of a series of one-paragraph, persuasive essays, but you may choose to do something different. Specific review and guidelines for the exam will be offered later; now students will begin working on the essay format.

The one-paragraph, persuasive essay has three parts: the thesis statement, the supporting evidence, and the conclusion. The writer's goal in the essay is to persuade the reader that a certain point of view is correct. This point of view is stated directly in the first sentence and serves as a summary of the argument that will be developed in the rest of the paragraph.

5. **Offer** the following examples of a thesis statement:
   - Freud was a psychologist.
   - Jack represents id.
   - Golding believes that mankind's basic nature is destructive.
   - Golding had many interesting views about mankind.

6. **Ask** which of these are not effective thesis statements. Discuss why. (The first one because it is a fact that most people would not dispute and the fourth one because it is too general. The other two examples are better because they clearly state a specific position that can be argued.)

7. **Elicit** and discuss the validity of other possible thesis statements that relate to the novel.

8. **Remind** students that thesis statements never begin with such verbose openings as "I think," "In my opinion," or combinations of these irrelevant openings such as "I believe that in my opinion…"

9. **Explain** that the group will practice developing thesis statements related to Golding's use of weather in Chapter 9.

10. **Have** students reread the first paragraph on page 166, marking or listing phrases that help them visualize the setting and that create a particular mood. (e.g., revolving piles of gas piled up, colors drained from water and trees.)

11. **Discuss** the passage:
    - What mood is Golding trying to create? (The mood is oppressive. Golding uses images of oppressive heat. He also uses colorless images to highlight the black mass of the flies.)
    - How else does Golding use weather imagery throughout the chapter? (From p. 174 to the end, Golding uses negative storm imagery [e.g., "between the flashes of lightning the air was dark and terrible"] to highlight the violence that is breaking out that is based on the dark and horrible part of mankind's nature.)

12. **Have** students write thesis statements about Golding's use of weather within the chapter.

13. **Discuss** the strengths and weaknesses of these thesis statements using the following criteria:
    - Was the topic an opinion that can be defended?
    - Was it specific enough?
    - Was it well written?

14. **Have** a student read the paragraph on page 170 when Piggy and Ralph arrive at the party.

15. **Discuss** the passage:
    - Describe what Ralph and Piggy saw when entering the party. (The boys are almost finished eating. They are lying about, laughing and singing. They all seem to be having fun—as Jack promised. Jack is painted and garlanded like an idol. Around him are piles of meat, fruit, and coconut shells of water.)
    - Compare the image of Jack at the feast with the image of the pig's head on the stick that was sacrificed to the beast. How would Freud explain this comparison? (Both the beast and Jack are being worshipped by the boys. Golding compares Jack to an idol. Around Jack are offerings, much like the offering made to the beast. Freud would say that both Jack and the beast are appealing to the boys' primal instincts and, that in this idolizing, the boys are turning to a savage, tribal way of worshipping. They are thus turning further away from civilization.)

16. **Have** students break into two groups: one assuming the role of Jack and the other the role of Ralph. Have each group develop an expanded version of the boy's speech to the group in convincing them which tribe to join. Each group should have a group member deliver the speech. Students should vote as themselves and then as their characters for which tribe they would join.

17. **Discuss** the differences in their votes. (Ralph's appeal should be based on responsibility to the group—building shelters and keeping the rescue fire going. He could use guilt as a device to motivate the boys. Jack's appeal should be based on hunting, fun, and fear of the beast.)

18. **Discuss** Simon's role:
    • Has Simon's role evolved since the group discussed his role at the beginning of the novel? Does he share in mankind's essential illness? (Simon has become the truth teller of the group, telling the boys what they don't want to hear. On p. 98, he tells the boys the beast is "us," but they don't respond. On p. 146, he suggests they go to the place where the beast was spotted to check to see what is there, but the boys again ignore him. He has also been the one motivated by being good, helping the littluns to get fruit [p. 59], building the shelters, protecting Piggy [pp. 43, 74]. He seems to be motivated solely by good behavior as if he is not touched by mankind's essential illness.)
    • Why does Golding refer to Simon as the beast (p. 175)? Compare Sam and Eric's description of the beast on page 112 with Golding's description of the mob destroying Simon. Is the comparison ironic? (Golding calls Simon the beast because this is how the boys see him during their frenzy. Moreover, Golding's description of the boys matches Sam and Eric's description of the beast—both are said to have teeth and claws. Both are said to attack. It is ironic that Simon is called the beast when he is coming to tell the boys the truth about the beast, but they destroy him while ignoring his attempt to tell the truth.)

19. **Have** a student read aloud the last paragraph on pages 175–176 and the last paragraph at the end of the chapter on page 177.

20. **Discuss** the passages:
    • What is happening in each paragraph? (The paratrooper, having had his strings freed by Simon, is carried out to sea. Simon's body also is carried out to sea.)
    • What do these events both have to do with the boys finding out the truth about what Sam and Eric saw? (Now the boys cannot know the truth. The paratrooper is gone so they cannot confront the truth, and Simon is gone so they cannot hear the truth.)
    • What kind of imagery does Golding use to describe Simon's body going out to sea? Why does he choose this kind of image? (After the storm, the image is extremely peaceful. Simon is described as silver and marble

and the luminescence around his head is reminiscent of an angel's halo. Golding describes the leaving as gentle and solitary in contrast to the savagery of the murderous mob.)

HOMEWORK

Students should complete the following:

Read the excerpt from Journal/Blog Entry 4 that is included at the end of this chapter. Write the fourth journal entry using the following guidelines:

Guidelines for Journal/Blog Entry 4: Simon Said

1. Describe your role in Simon's death.
   a. Begin with a description of the weather and what you were doing just before Simon appeared.
   b. Use violent storm imagery to create the mood.
2. What were you doing just before Simon appeared?
   a. Were you participating in the dance?
   b. What were you thinking/feeling?
3. How did you feel when "the beast" appeared? Did you know it was Simon?
4. Describe the attack of the beast.
   a. Focus on your role.
   b. If you were id-driven, focus on the primal emotions that were driving your actions.

Read and annotate Chapters 10 and 11.

Lesson 11: Chapters 10 and 11—The Triumph of Id

PROCEDURE

1. **Have** students summarize a few specific passages from the chapter that they think are particularly representative of Freud's theory. Allow other students to agree with or dispute the proffered connections between the passages and the personality aspect in Freud's theory.

2. **Have** a few students read aloud and explicate an excerpt from their character's journal entry 4.

3. **Elicit** a definition of a thesis statement. (Usually the first sentence or two in an essay, it tells the opinion that the writer will defend throughout the rest of the paragraph.)

4. **Explain** that as students discuss the remainder of the book, they also will discuss how to support a thesis statement. To do this, students will first need to review an aspect of Freud's theory that has probably been explained though several students' PowerPoint presentations: ego defense mechanisms. This will give them more options for defending their thesis statements.

5. **Elicit** a general definition of ego defense mechanisms. (When the reality of a situation makes it too difficult for the ego to maintain a balance between the id and the super-ego, it turns to a defense mechanism to cope. Although this strategy might be effective in the short term, over time, maintaining the false explanation usually becomes too emotionally demanding.)

6. **Elicit** definitions for *rationalization* and *denial*. (If these have not been discussed previously, define these defense mechanisms and elicit examples from Chapter 10.)

   • Rationalization—focusing on ersatz, more-palatable explanations for unacceptable behaviors instead of the real explanation (e.g., Piggy blaming Simon's murder on the darkness, the thunder and lightning, and the dance—he calls it an accident rather than a murder).

   • Denial—arguing that a stressful event doesn't exist (e.g., Piggy telling Ralph that Simon might still be alive).

7. **Explain** that students are going to compare the reactions of Ralph, Piggy, and Jack to Simon's death and that they should try to include discussions of the characters' use of defense mechanisms in these comparisons.

8. **Assign** the parts of narrator, Ralph, and Piggy. Use the reader's theatre technique to read from the top of page 180 to the middle of page 181 where Piggy shakes his head.

9. **Discuss** the passage:

- What is Ralph's reaction to Simon's death? (Ralph calls Simon's death murder. He is stricken by what happens and argues that he has some responsibility for it.)
- How would Freud explain Ralph's response? (Freud would say that Ralph feels guilt or shame because his super-ego tells him what he did was wrong. This is why Ralph feels both stricken and has a sense of loathing. This is also why he is frightened "of us" (p. 181). He acts out of his id and this loss of control, which resulted in a "kind of feverish excitement" (p. 180) that scares Ralph.
- What is Piggy's response to Simon's death? (Piggy cannot face the fact that Simon was murdered and is thus in denial. He makes excuses for— or rationalizes—the group's violence, blaming Simon, then the weather. He wants to deny that he or Ralph were even involved in the dance.)
- How would Freud explain Piggy's response? (Freud would say that Piggy is engaged in defense mechanisms because the reality that the group is capable of murder is too much for him to accept. His super-ego is so strong that this violation of rules is beyond what his ego can handle, so he makes up excuses.)

10. **Assign** the parts of narrator, Jack, and someone to read the lines that are not attributed to a specifically named boy. Use the reader's theatre technique to read from the bottom of page 184 when the chief pauses to the middle of page 185 when Jack explains that you can't tell what the beast might do.

11. **Discuss** the passage:
- What is Jack's response to Simon's death? (Jack uses the death as an opportunity to aggrandize the beast. He admits that someone who looked like Simon was beaten in what appeared to be a killing; however, the beast has the ability to disguise himself as a boy and the beast cannot be killed. As Golding states, this further terrorizes the boys. Therefore, Jack has used the death to add to his own importance in protecting the tribe from this increasingly powerful beast.)
- How would Freud explain Jack's response? (Freud would say that Jack uses the death to increase his own power and to justify his own increasingly aggressive behavior. Jack admits that the beast is unpredictable [p. 185] not realizing that the beast is his own unchecked id.)

12. **Ask** each student to write a thesis statement in response to the following prompt: "Compare and contrast Jack and Piggy's response to Simon's death." Have several students share their statements. Select one to be developed into a paragraph.

13. **Have** half of the students generate lists of ways in which the responses are similar. Have the other half generate a list of ways in which these responses contrast with each other.

14. **Explain** the following guidelines for developing the body of the paragraph:
    1. Content must be drawn from the text or other sources, but cannot reflect the writer's opinion.
    2. All sentences must relate back to the thesis statement.
    3. The body of the paragraph cannot contain another thesis.
    4. The final sentence should explain how the body of the paragraph supports the thesis statement.

15. **Have** students use their lists to develop the thesis statement into a paragraph either comparing the boys' responses or contrasting them. Use the guidelines to discuss some of the paragraphs. An example follows. (Both Jack's and Piggy's response to Simon's death fail to deal with the reality or the consequences of the situation. Piggy tries to rationalize what happened. He blames the time of day, the weather, and the dance. He then suggests that Simon might not even be dead. Finally, he denies that it was murder, calling it an accident, then refusing to continue the discussion. Similarly, Jack makes up irrational reasons for what happened. He claims the beast was in disguise as Simon, thus also suggesting that Simon is not dead. He also claims that they beat the beast but did not kill it. Thus, neither boy admits to what happened, nor does either boy accept any responsibility for Simon's death.)

16. **Assign** the parts of narrator, Roger, Robert, Jack, and someone to read the lines that are not attributed to a specified boy. Use the reader's theatre technique to read from the break on the bottom of page 184 to when Jack explains that the boys with Ralph are spoilers.

17. **Discuss** the passage:
    - How would you characterize Jack's behavior in this passage? (He has become paranoid and irrationally cruel. We see his sadistic side escalate as he plans violence against other boys. He has prepared a deadly weapon against anyone who might be considered an intruder, although only Ralph, Piggy, Sam, and Eric are outside of the area. He hurts Wilfred for no explainable reason.)
    - Why does Jack call the boys who remain with Ralph spoilers? How does this parallel what the beast had said to Simon about stopping the rest of the boys from having fun? (Jack needs to respond to the boy who asks why the boys with Ralph would want to sneak in. He wants to devalue the outsiders to make it OK to hurt them. He still sees them as a threat to his power—or a super-ego-based threat to his id.)

It is here that I make a connection to Hitler's treatment of the Jews and other minority groups. Hitler needed to make the Jews seem less than human so that the German people would be more accepting of the inhumane treatment that he had planned. Most bullies devalue their opponents rather than their opponent's ideas, as do Jack and Hitler. I then guide students to make connections between the book and other dictators. Should this be appropriate to your unit, this is the time to make this connection.

18. **Discuss** page 192:
    - Piggy says the beast is real. Is he correct? How would both Golding and Freud answer this question? (Yes, the beast is real in that it is what Golding refers to as "mankind's essential illness" [p. 98], or the savagery that is at people's core. Piggy's reference to the beast having come means that an actual monster has come, not Jack. Still, he is correct in that Jack has come and Jack is the beast driven by his savagery, or what Freud would call id unchecked by super-ego.
    - What does the destruction of the shelter represent? (The shelters represent civilization, or super-ego, as they are the fruition of the long-term goal to protect the boys against inevitable bad weather. The destruction of the hut represents id's destruction of one of the last remaining symbols of super-ego.)

19. **Assign** the roles of narrator, Piggy, Sam, and Ralph. Use the reader's theatre technique to read from the bottom of page 196 where Piggy discusses the ordinary fire to the middle of page 198 where Sam explains that Jack will be painted.

20. **Discuss** the passage:
    - Throughout the passage, Piggy focuses on logic and rules. What are some examples of this? (He still seems unable to understand why they can't keep the fire going even though it seems to be the only way to get rescued. He still wants to use the conch to maintain proper order during conversation. Moreover, Piggy presents the logical argument that he will use with Jack to retrieve his glasses and states that this argument is based on what is right.)
    - What would Freud say is the reason that Piggy maintains this line of reasoning? (Piggy maintains this line of reasoning because he is so entrenched in super-ego that he uses rules and logic in response to Jack's id-based behavior.)
    - Why does Piggy ask the boys to consider if they are savages? (He still doesn't fully grasp, or denies, that the boys are completely following Jack's desires to have fun and to ignore what is best for the group.)

- How does Ralph want to dress when they approach Jack's tribe? Contrast this to how Sam predicts Jack's tribe would be dressed. How would Freud explain the difference? (Ralph wants to clean up and present a semblance of civilization. Jack's tribe will be painted. Freud would explain that the clothing is an attempt to resurrect super-ego as it represents a return to civilization. Jack's tribe is painted because this represents their savagery that is driven by the id.)

- How does this last attempt to dress up follow the reoccurring use of clothing throughout the novel? Relate this to the plot graph. (Clothing has been a reoccurring symbol of civilization. As super-ego falls and id rises, clothing becomes more ruined, symbolizing the ruin of civilization and superego.)

21. **Discuss** Piggy's death:
    - Piggy's last comment is to ask which is better, rules or killing. Why doesn't this elicit the response Piggy wants? (Because it is too late to make a logical appeal as id is too dominant, but even at the end, Piggy doesn't understand that id is unstoppable.)

    - In the beginning of the book (p. 67), Roger cannot bring himself to hit the littluns with the rocks he throws at them. How would Freud explain the contrast between Roger killing Piggy and the earlier constrained rock throwing? (Earlier, Roger could not hit the littluns with the stones because he was still under the influence of laws, parents, and the limits or taboos of civilization. Now these limits are completely gone and he feels no shame or limits for his destructive behavior.)

    - What is the significance of the conch being shattered when Piggy is killed? (The conch represents order and is the symbol of the civilization that Piggy clings to at the end of his life. Jack, being representative of id, cannot be completely free of super-ego until both Piggy and the conch—both symbols of super-ego—are gone.)

If special arrangements need to be made to schedule the presentation of the mandatory/optional projects, now is the time to do so.

HOMEWORK

Students should complete the following:

Write a one-paragraph essay addressing the question, "Who is responsible for Piggy's death?"

Read and annotate the final chapter.

Lesson 12: Chapter 12—The End

PROCEDURE

1. **Review** and discuss several homework essays, checking to see that the essays begin with a clearly defined thesis statement and continue with support from the text. Collect and grade the essays, if you wish.

2. **Divide** the class into small groups. Have the groups imagine that they are a panel of officers on the rescue ship interviewing either Jack or Ralph about the events of the final days on the island. Have each group write five questions to ask its interviewee. Have two people role-play Jack and Ralph answering questions to each panel.

3. **Discuss** the following topics if they were not brought up during the role-play:

    *   Compare and contrast Ralph smashing the pig's head with Roger smashing the conch. (Both the conch and the Pig's head gleamed white and represented the driving force on the island at different times. The conch represented order and the pig's head represented mankind's essential illness. When Ralph broke the pig's head, it still seemed to grow bigger and to smile, suggesting that unlike the conch, it could not be destroyed.)

    *   What was Jack's ostensible reason for hunting Ralph? (Ralph was a spoiled who was dangerous.)

    *   What were Ralph's original plans to survive the hunt? (He wanted Sam and Eric to join him in fighting back. When they refused, he planned to hide in a thicket near Castle Rock and have Sam and Eric lead the tribe away from him.)

    *   Why didn't this plan work? (Someone overheard Sam and Eric talking to Ralph. Roger beat them into revealing Ralph's hiding place.)

    *   Why did Roger sharpen a stick at both ends? (The tribe planned to sacrifice Ralph to the beast as they had done with the boar.)

    *   On pages 226 and 227, Golding uses a great deal of animal imagery to describe Ralph? What are some of these images? Why did Golding use these images at this time? How would Freud explain Ralph's behavior? ("He squatted back on his heels and showed his teeth" [p. 226]; "launched himself like a cat; stabbed, snarling" [p. 226]; "he shied like a horse" [p. 227]. Golding is suggesting that Ralph is reverting to his basic instincts. Freud would say this is Ralph's id at work, driven by the survival instinct.)

    *   Why was it ironic that the ship came to the island because it saw the fire? (It was Jack who initially let the rescue fire go out and Jack who did not want to be rescued. The fire as a signal was Piggy and Ralph's plan. Yet, when Jack started the fire that was destroying the island, it actually brought the initial plan to fruition. Jack had no concern for

the destruction the fire would bring, only for his immediate goal of destroying Ralph. Yet, this destructive fire saved Ralph and led to the rescue. Moreover, it restored Ralph's leadership and ended Jack's power.)

- Why is it ironic that a war ship rescues the boys? (Because it saves the boys from the ravages of destruction on the island, but it also represents destruction in the larger world. This irony of this suggests that the boys cannot escape evil by leaving the island. Evil was not simply on the island because the boys lacked adult supervision. This ever-present destructive force is, as Golding continues to point out, mankind's essential illness.)
- What is the importance of the officer's uniform and questioning? (Clothing has been an ongoing symbol of civilization. The pristine uniform suggests the school uniform and order that began the book. Yet, it is also similar to the savages' paint because it is what the officer wears to do battle. His questioning is significant because it is reminiscent both of Jack's initial comment that they are English and not savages and of Piggy's initial desire to take names.)
- When the officer asks who is in charge, why does Ralph say he is and why does Jack not protest? (With the uniformed officer appearing on the island, super-ego is restored and this limit's Jack's id to the point where his power is checked. He can no longer command the destruction and thus is no longer chief. Ralph and ego are returned to prominence because sense [reason] has returned to the island.)
- Why is Ralph no longer innocent at the end of the chapter? (Because he is now aware of mankind's potential for destruction.)

HOMEWORK

Students should complete the following:

Read the Excerpt From Journal/Blog Entry 5 that is included at the end of this chapter. Write the fifth journal entry using the following guidelines:

Guidelines for Journal/Blog Entry 5: Ralph

1. Write about the hunt for Ralph.
   a. Describe the preparation for the hunt and the actual hunt.
   b. Stop with the arrival of the officer.
2. Focus on the building emotion as well as the events. Therefore, include your character's emotional responses.
3. Include the following:
   a. Imagery to reflect the mood (e.g., animal and dark imagery)
   b. Symbolic acts and objects
   c. Strong voice

Lesson 13: Review

At the beginning of this lesson, you should explain the format that you have chosen for the final. I have found that, for this unit, two formats work well: an open-book, take-home exam and an open-book, in-school exam. I usually let the students decide which they prefer, although the latter takes 2 days, with two questions per day. Time constraints do not always allow for this to take place. As this is often students' most content-rich unit, they typically seem anxious about the exam; therefore, I am explicit about what content, format, and questions will be on the test.

PROCEDURE

1. **Have** a few students read aloud and discuss an excerpt from their character's final entry.
2. **Distribute** the following list of topics that students will review for the final (or choose your own):

Study Topics: *Lord of the Flies* Final Examination

- The development of evil and the fall of reason on the island.
- Freud's explanation for the above.
- Golding's use of imagery to enhance the mood.
- Golding's use of repeated symbols.
- The island as a metaphor for mankind's essential illness.
- The boys as an allegory for Freud's theory.
- The beast and the chief.

3. **Review** the topics, eliciting various thesis statements and related support for each one.
    - **The development of evil and the fall of reason on the island.** (Key points: The boys start out civilized with meetings and rules. They make plans for the group good and set long-term goals. Over time, each killing of the pig becomes less difficult, each death of a boy becomes more premeditated, and group goals are abandoned for hunting and fun. Cruelty takes on an ever-increasing role. Finally, through hunting and fire, the boys are destroying their means of survival because they forsake the long-term consequences of their behavior to achieve an immediate goal—hunting Ralph.)
    - **Freud's explanation for the above.** (Key points: People are born with an id that is concerned with survival and immediate needs. It is self-

ish, illogical, and animalistic. By age 6 or so, people should develop a super-go that is an internalization of societal and parental values. It redirects a person's energy into long-term goals that benefit the group. The ego is our self-concept that we use to weigh and resolve continual conflicts between the two. Id, being the one aspect that is inborn, is the most powerful of the three and, therefore, will usually triumph over the other two.)

- **Golding's use of imagery to enhance the mood.** (Key points: Golding uses both light and dark descriptive images, as well as animal images, to reflect and enhance the mood of text passages. When the passage is focused on mankind's illness or on danger, the settling is described as dark, mysterious, and often animalistic. In these passages, the weather is often foreboding. When the boys are civilized or good the imagery is usually light, pretty, and colorful.)

- **Golding's use of repeated symbols.** (Key points: The conch represents order and civilization. Clothing does also, but the former is destroyed in a final dramatic moment and the latter decays over time, mirroring the boys' descent into savagery. The officer's uniform represents both war and civilization. The shelters represent long-term goals and are finally destroyed as long-term goals are abandoned. The fire is the most complex symbol as it represents the long-term, group goal of rescue but, when out of control, it represents violence and destruction. Thus, it represents the complete personality; when controlled it is beneficial, but when out of control, it is destructive.)

- **The island as a metaphor for mankind's essential illness.** (Key points: The island is a miniature version of what is happening in the larger world. The forces of evil in man have brought about war and have brought about the savagery in the tribe. The savagery on the island in not due to lack of adult supervision because adults also fall prey to their essential illness. Moreover, the structure of the island represents a personality: the beach is light, orderly, and safe, but the jungle is dangerous and dark. The beach washes away as the savagery expands.)

- **The boys as an allegory for Freud's theory.** (Piggy represents super-ego. He has internalized his auntie's rules and does not break them, even when doing so would not lead to negative consequences. He continually shows concern for the long-term good of the group. Jack, in contrast to Piggy, represents id. In the beginning, when he is limited by Ralph, he brings food to the group and ensures its survival. In time, he reveals himself to be completely selfish and wants no part of rules that benefit the group. Rather, he insists on rules that benefit him. He shows no concern for long-term goals or the group and strives to eliminate anything that limits his power. Ralph is the balance between the two, wanting to have fun and to be rescued. He establishes rules, but remains reasonable and is open to opportunities for fun. He often reasons things out in situations when Jack has a visceral or illogical response.)

- **The beast and the chief.** (Key points: The destruction of society, whether in the world at large, or on the island, has its roots in man's destructive nature. The beast is not a monster that is separate from man, but an integral part of his nature. It is what Golding refers to as mankind's essential illness. Thus, as is often stated in the book, the beast is "us." Moreover, as the pig's head tells Simon, it is not something that can be hunted and killed. Therefore, when faced with a choice between civilization and savagery, the beast in the boys always triumphs and chooses savagery.

-      Ralph is elected chief because he has the conch and represents societies rules, but this victory of rules is short lived. Jack later becomes chief of his own tribe that focuses on fun and hunting with no concern for the long-term needs of the group. This soon becomes a tribe completely subject to and at the mercy of Jack's cruelty. Jack is called "a proper chief" when he develops a means of killing any of the outsiders who are the last vestiges of civilization. This shows that mankind's essential illness is in charge.)

HOMEWORK

Students should complete the following:

Study for the final if it is to be given in school or complete the final as a take-home examination.

Turn in completed maps with the final.

Lesson 14: Project Time

PROCEDURE

1. **Review** graded final exams if desired.
2. **Have** students evaluate the unit by discussing all or some of the following questions:
   - What did you like best about the unit?
   - What was the most challenging part?
   - What did you like about Freud's theory? Do you think it is valid?
   - What did you like or dislike about the novel? Would you recommend it? Why or why not?
   - How would you change the unit for future classes?
   - How would you evaluate your participation in the unit?

3. **Have** students present their final mandatory/optional projects.

Challenging Minds: Highlighted Activities

Following is a list of activities used in this unit that can be adapted to many instructional and enrichment situations to complement a variety of student strengths.

1. **Journals/blogs:** I start having students keep journals as actual historical characters in third grade where each child in the class is assigned the role of a person who sailed to Jamestown. Students then post podcasts, reading excerpts from their journal as "News of the Day—1609 Edition." In fifth grade, students keep journals as citizens of a Virginia town torn between allegiances to the North and the South. I prefer, in these kinds of projects, to use minor characters: a thatcher instead of John Smith or one of the choir members instead of Jack. Creating a famous person's or a main character's blog would present interesting challenges; however, using the history or the novel's details as a base for bringing dimension to a new character keeps the focus on the time period or the story, and is a very different challenge from blogging as a character about whom much personal information is provided.

2. **Formal essays:** Many bright students struggle with using text and research to detail their opinion. They prefer, instead, simply to offer their first thoughts or to go off on tangents. This strategy, because of the strength of their initial reactions, has worked well for many of them in earlier grades. Focusing on one thesis statement requires a certain intellectual discipline that these students need to develop. I have used the above instruction on developing a thesis in a variety of classes and grade levels, always with the caveat "back it up from the text; what you have said is your opinion." This can frustrate some gifted students, but it will become increasingly more important as they move to higher grades.

3. **Reader's theatre:** Whether teaching a fantasy in fifth grade or *Lord of the Flies* in eighth, I find this technique brings a passage to life and works especially well for students who have a strength in understanding characters' interpersonal and intrapersonal aspects.

4. **Maps:** Many novels, particularly in the beginning, offer a great many details about setting and locations that are integral to understanding the story. The neighborhood in Harper Lee's *To Kill a Mocking Bird* and the land of Prydian in Lloyd Alexander's *The Black Cauldron* are good examples. Visualizing the setting and the relationships of different parts of the setting to each other is both challenging and important. I often begin by having students create and compare maps. They then edit their own maps in light of what their peers have included in theirs. Students can continue to embellish the maps as they read and I give a final grade at the end of the unit. One warning: Don't have them color in the maps until the end as this makes it difficult to include additional features later in the unit.

Adaptations

1. *Lord of the Flies* is my favorite unit to teach in junior high. Students at this age always respond well to the self-reflection aspect of Freud's theory, finding it a way to understand both their own milieu and the larger world. If time is a major constraint on being able to implement this unit, shorter books could be substituted. My first recommendation as either a replacement or as a follow-up would be *Strange Case of Dr. Jekyll and Mr. Hyde* by Robert Louis Stevenson, another novel that explores the duality of good and evil in human nature (and it was the putative inspiration for the Hulk).

2. There are two film adaptations of *Lord of the Flies*—a 1963 version, directed by Peter Brook, and a 1990 version, directed by Harry Hook. The former is vastly superior to the latter. The background of the making of the film is almost as interesting as the book itself. One could do the entire unit using this film, disregarding the book, but keeping most of the lessons offered above.

3. More could be made of social studies connections to the novel. I always tie in the Nazi regime and WWII. Often, while I do this unit, the classroom teacher is teaching *The Diary of a Young Girl* by Anne Frank. We then bring all of the students together for a final discussion of good and evil in human nature. Many other social studies and current events projects can be connected to the Freudian aspects of this unit.

4. Much has been written about the social-emotional needs of gifted children. This unit provides several opportunities for students to reflect on their own feelings by discussing issues such as Jack's bullying, Piggy being an outsider, and the choir's unquestioning following of Jack's lead.

5. Finally, here is a list of other books that could be analyzed from a Freudian perspective, either as a substitute or a complement to *Lord of the Flies*:
   - *Night* by Elie Wiesel
   - *Macbeth* by William Shakespeare
   - *Lord of the Rings* by J. R. R. Tolkien
   - *Green Boy* by Susan Cooper
   - *The Hunger Games* by Suzanne Collins
   - *The Cat in the Hat* by Dr. Seuss
   - *Treasure Island* by Robert Louis Stevenson

Sigmund Freud's Biography
(GREY, 1998; WOLLHEIM, 1971)

Sigmund Freud was born May 6, 1856, in Moravia (which was, at the time, part of the Austrian Empire) to Jewish parents. His father was a struggling wool merchant and 20 years older than his mother. Sigmund was the oldest of eight children and displayed an outstanding intellect at an early age. Therefore, his parents, although impoverished, did all that they could to provide him with a good education.

When Sigmund was a young boy, his father lost the family business and eventually moved the family to Vienna, the capital of Austria, where Sigmund grew up. He graduated high school with honors and eventually went to medical school—one of the few career paths available to Austrian Jews at the time. There, he concentrated his studies on neurophysiology, which taught the prevailing belief that the only forces active within the human body were physical-chemical ones. In 1881, the same year in which he would graduate from medical school, he met Martha Bernays. Freud began courting her in earnest. Two months later, they became engaged, but because of Freud's poverty, they kept the engagement a secret. They waited 4 years to marry—until Freud was able to support a family ("Young Dr. Freud," 2002).

After graduation, he directed a children's ward in Berlin for a short time. He then returned to Vienna and set up a private practice in neurology and neuropsychiatry. He began treating neurotic patients with hypnosis, but soon abandoned this treatment method for what became known as the "talking cure." This talking cure had its roots in a patient of his mentor, Josef Breuer. This patient was a 21-year-old woman known as Anna O. Anna had spent much of her own life caring for her father. She first developed a cough for which her doctor could find no physical cause. She then began talking only in English rather than her native German. After her father died, Anna refused to eat, developed a loss of feeling in her hands and feet, suffered from vision problems, and began having involuntary spasms. Moreover, she began suffering from fantasies, mood swings, and often attempted suicide. Doctors could find no physical causes for this set of symptoms.

Breuer diagnosed Anna as suffering from hysteria (which psychologists now call conversion disorder). At night, Anna would fall into trance-like states that Breuer called "spontaneous hypnosis." During these trances, she often could explain her daytime problems. She typically reported feeling better after explaining the roots of her behaviors. Breuer sometimes saw a connection between her explanations and particular symptoms. In one notable example, she described her disgust at seeing a woman drinking from a glass out of which a dog had recently drunk. Shorty after seeing this episode, Anna refused to drink. But after retelling the episode during one of her trances, she no longer experienced an aversion to drinking.

Later, Breuer and Freud wrote a book in which they explained hysteria as the result of a person experiencing a traumatic event that is in extreme conflict with his or her understanding of the world—or what the world should be. Although the emotions associated with the experiences are repressed, they do not go away. The patient expresses them in a way vaguely related to the experience. When the patient is made aware of the association between the original experience and the symptom—as through the talking cure—the unexpressed emotion and the symptom go away.

In March 1938, the Nazi army regime annexed Austria to Germany with little opposition. This led to immediate and violent demonstrations of anti-Semitism. Soon after the annexation, Freud's daughter, Anna, was arrested and questioned by the Gestapo and valuables were taken from his home. Although the Nazis strictly controlled Jewish emigration, Freud and his immediate family—with the help of luminaries such as Princess Marie Bonaparte and American Ambassador W. C. Bullit—immigrated to England. His sisters were not as fortunate, however, and later perished in Nazi concentration camps. Freud continued to live and work in England where he later died from a protracted battle with smoking-related cancer of his mouth and jaw.

Sigmund Freud's Theory

LEVELS OF CONSCIOUSNESS (FREUD, 1961, 1989)

It was experiences with patients like Anna O. that inspired Freud to develop his theory of the conscious and unconscious mind—an idea that he did not invent, but certainly popularized. Freud described the *conscious* as what one is aware of at any particular moment. Ideas can move in and out of the conscious mind as a person's intellectual focus changes. The *preconscious* is closely related to the conscious. It includes any information that can readily be brought to the conscious as a person's focus changes to new topics.

These two aspects of the mind are small in comparison to what Freud detailed as the *unconscious*. This aspect of the mind includes all of the information, motivations (or compulsions), desires, and instincts (or drives) that are not readily available to be brought into the conscious mind. Some things, such as instincts or drives (e.g., for food and sex), are born there.

Other things, such as memories of traumatic experiences and the ensuing emotions associated with these experiences, are placed there because they are too difficult for the conscious mind to deal with. Therefore, things that fit into this aspect of consciousness often are denied or repressed and are brought to the forefront of the mind as disguised thought and behavior. Freud explained that a person defensively places these traumatic memories and emotions into the unconscious mind when the realities of the event are in extreme conflict with the person's attitudes and values. Such memories, although stored in the unconscious, may have a tremendous impact on behavior. An example of this would be Anna O.'s refusal to drink.

ID, EGO, AND SUPER-EGO (FREUD, 1989, 1990A, 1990B)

Freud eventually modified the levels of consciousness theory to accommodate the theoretical concepts of the id, ego, and super-ego. According to Freud, the ego is housed in the conscious mind, the superego in the preconscious, and the ever-powerful id in the unconscious. It is these three aspects of the psyche that are central to this unit's analysis of the novel.

Human beings—like other animals—are born with drives to survive (actualized through aggression) and reproduce. To assure these ends, from birth, our nervous systems are programmed to guide us to eat, drink, and eventually engage in sex. The drives to fulfill these basic needs are founded in the unconscious and are collectively called the *id*. The id, in and of itself, is not—as some people think—a bad thing. Left unfulfilled, these needs only grow stronger and more consuming. We are born this way, and it is a good thing, as the satisfaction of basic needs leads to survival and reproduction. Picture an infant. It is consumed by taking care of immediate needs with no concern for consequences; the infant is born knowing what it wants to survive (i.e., food and liquids) and wanting them immediately. He or she is not concerned with waiting for gratification or taking turns. It is this immediacy that can be argued is central to the survival of our species—as it is for other species as well.

Survival and reproduction, while essential for all species, are not the only aspects of people's makeup. We also have a moral side that resides in our *super-ego*. (Although the super-ego is the third aspect of the personality to develop, following the ego, I define it second because it seems easiest to understand as direct opposition to the id.) The super-ego grows out of a child's learning through experience that not all desires can be obtained, and those that can be obtained cannot always be fulfilled instantly. Basically, the super-ego is a person's internalization of parental and societal values of what is right and wrong. It stores these values as rules and uses anxiety or guilt to enforce them. When a person breaks a rule, anxiety sets in because the child feels that the parents will disapprove of or punish the behavior. Collectively, these rules are the conscience that strives for, but probably does not achieve, perfect behavior.

The super-ego should start to become evident by age 5. A child who has not developed a super-ego by age 7 or so may learn to be afraid of consequences, but probably will not develop this internalized set of rules. The issue becomes confounded when the family and society have nontraditional values, as in Nazi Germany, and a child's super-ego is based on a set of evil standards.

The super-ego operates in direct contradiction to the id. While the id operates according to the *pleasure principle*, the super-ego operates according to the *morality principle*. Maintaining the balance between these two forces is the job of the *ego*.

Ego is our sense of self as we fit into the larger world. According to Freud, it is this sense of self that is the judge or moderator, striving to balance the needs of the super-ego and the id, guiding the impulsivity of the id into a socially acceptable manner. Preferably, the ego will guide the desires of the id into directions that will make the person happy and at the same time benefit the larger group. For example, aggression may be channeled into sports, or the desire to go to a party may be postponed until after studying. This latter example is called *delayed gratification*. It is possible, however, that the ego decides on socially acceptable behavior that does not truly satisfy the whole personality—such as entering into a job that is not personally rewarding.

If a person sees him- or herself as religious, family orientated, popular, or smart, then that person uses these qualities to weigh the consequences and benefits of acting upon a desire. This is how a person balances the often-competing needs of the id and super-ego, using a sense of self as the judge. I often summarize this balancing act as the angel and devil that appear arguing on Homer Simpson's or Bugs Bunny's shoulder. Ego is guided by the *reality principle*. Students need to see that the perception of reality differs among and with groups. They can all recall experiences in their lives when people retold the same events differently—with each believing he or she had the correct version of events.

Growing out of the ego are a series of *defense mechanisms,* tools that the ego has for defending itself against realities that are too difficult to bear or for which the super-ego will dispense too much guilt. All, except sublimation—redirecting the impulse into socially acceptable outlets—are harmful in the long run because they take mental energy to maintain the defensive facade. This can be seen in Anna O. Although she repressed the initial episode, expending mental energy required to repress the event and the related emotions exacted its price: her neurotic behavior.

Students must remember that no aspect is good or bad in and off itself: each can be taken to the extreme. An extreme id is too caught up in immediate gratification and has no sense of consequences. Even by eighth grade, most students see this kind of person as scary. On the other hand, an extreme super-ego is quite rigid and may be too insufferable to be around or to ever have fun.

The final point that I make with students about Freud is the open-ended interpretation of his views on sublimation. Is it a good thing for a person to constantly redirect desires into socially acceptable ways. If one desires to be a poet, but ends up pleasing the family and becomes a doctor, society may benefit, but will the person wake up one day and realize that true happiness has been elusive? The literature is not clear on what Freud would recommend.

Name: _____ Date: _____

Lord of the Flies **Grading Sheet**

1. Discussion   _____/75

2. Map   _____/10

3. PowerPoint presentation   _____/75

4. Mandatory/optional project(s)   _____/75

5. Annotation   _____/25

6. Journal/blog entries   _____/40

7. Final   _____/100

Total: _____/400

Name: _____ Date: _____

Lord of the Flies Final Exam

No answer should be longer than one paragraph. Remember, begin with a thesis statement, support this statement with the text and ancillary materials, and make sure that the connection between the thesis and the support is evident.

1. At the end of the novel, Ralph is no longer innocent. Why? According to Golding only, how did Ralph lose his innocence?
2. How does Freud's theory of personality support or contradict Golding's point of view?

Answer two of the questions below:

3. Discuss how the conch and the pig's head complement and contrast each other to represent the total condition on the island.
4. Pick one of the following symbols and explain what it symbolizes. Pick two points in the book to illustrate how the symbol evolves/develops:
   - fire
   - clothing
   - the beach
   - the shelters

5. Is there a beast on the island? How would both Golding and Freud answer this question?
6. Pick one of the main characters—Simon, Piggy, or Ralph—and explain why Jack would want that boy to die.

Answer the question below:

7. Briefly, in no more than two sentences, discuss the irony of one of the following:
   - the fact that the boys are rescued by a military officer
   - the final fire
   - the fact that Piggy wears glasses

Extra credit: Name another book that could be used to illustrate Freud's theory. Briefly, explain how it does so.

Journal/Blog Samples

EXCERPT FROM JOURNAL/BLOG ENTRY 1: INTRODUCING YOUR CHARACTER AND THE FIRST MEETING

We all live (lived I guess) in a small-like house 'bout ten miles outside London. It would be fine for a normal family but gets tight with nine people in it. My three older brothers are all dino-like huge with smaller brains. My older sister and mom keep out of their way and take care of my younger brother and sister. My dad isn't home too much; he works overtime at the factory. School never was too hard 'til my teacher sent in a poem I wrote to a fancy school. They sent back an invitation to attend the school for free and a one-way train ticket into London. When my teacher came to talk to my parents 'bout my attending The Roses—that's the name of the school—my father didn't care long as it was free. He was probably happy cause that meant one less mouth to feed at home. My mom didn't say nuthin'. My brothers thought it was funny that the school was called The Roses. Thought it was all fancy-like and girly-like. They also thought that going to school far away was stupid. They think that learning comes after eating, wrestling, and pretty much everything else. When my mom tucked me in that night she said it was all gonna be okay, that she's so proud of her little boy that's smart enough to go to a special school in London. It made me so happy that I slept like a log even thought I share a bed with little Eddie and he kicks. It made all the stuff my brothers say okay. . . .

When I got off the plane, I was so tired from struggling to get off and the air was so warm that I fell straight asleep. When I woke up, the first thing I noticed was the oppressive heat. It clung to me and pressured me to take off the bright red blazer and knee-high stockings that were my uniform at The Roses. Once I got that done, I started to wander. The sand squished between my toes. I'd only been to the beach once and this sensation brought memories of that day rushing back. The floor of the jungle was all crazy-like with trees and leaves everywhere. I wandered for awhile and got nowhere, the jungle all looked alike. Jungle walking made me hungry, thirsty, and tired; there was a low piece of granite sticking out of the ground. I sat for a minute and looked around. From there, I went in a very different direction trying to find something that wasn't really found in England.

—Leah N., eighth grade

EXCERPT FROM JOURNAL/BLOG ENTRY 2: YOUR REACTION TO THE JUNGLE

I marched along in time with the monkey's yells, and soaked up the place. I was at the pool before I knew it and sat down on the white rock partly covered in light green moss. At my feet, an ant was leading its band in a zigzag path across the lush grass. I played with the insects for a while, blocking off one path and then the other, leading them in a circle. The few trees surrounding the pool threw gorgeous shadows across the water, dancing like graceful eagles circling each other, slightly dangerous, yet in a remote, beautiful way. I slid quickly into the pond, breaking the surface and sending prisms of light scattering through the air. As my head came out of the water, there was an instant of pure perfection. The sun shone all around, just warm enough to keep the water from being uncomfortable. The forest smelled of fresh green growing things. Even though I didn't immediately see any animals, the jungle somehow seemed alive, its heart beating in a lively Cajun melody, harmonizing with itself. And then I saw the bird that I had somehow identified as *mine*: the huge creature which spread rainbows with its wings. It flapped and called out, its harsh screech strangely melodic. And then, once again, time returned to normal, leaving me in an ordinary paradise. I swam back and forth, taking joy in the cool water flowing across my parched skin. It was close to a half-hour before I clambered out and returned to the beach. As I walked back, I noted the careful order and precedence of the creatures of the jungle. The ants followed their leader, the baboons their alpha male. The jungle was filled with silent, powerful laws, which were never broken. My good mood was shattered, however, by my arrival at the beach.

—Tyce W., eighth grade

EXCERPT FROM JOURNAL/BLOG ENTRY 3: CHOOSING SIDES

This island is hell on earth. First, I get stuck here with a bunch of little horrors. The heat boils the blood beneath my skin every day. The sordid fruit makes my tongue shrivel and curl away. Then, it split. I hate Jack. I despise *Chief.* Which do I choose? The humiliation Jack felt during the assembly turned him away from the others. Now I have to choose. The choice is like the thunder and lightning that cracks and rolls above my head. Except that I have to choose; I can't just be in both crews. I would make my own group, but I would end up being hunted, what with my infamous character on the island.

Crack! Ralph hasn't forced me into anything. Jack is a complete parasite throughout the time here. *Crack!* The blue-white light shot across the black sky. Ralph has a sense of rescue. I don't know why; rescue probably won't happen any time soon, or at all. *Crack!* The lightning scar streaks across the heavens. Ralph knows common sense too.

Boom! The thunder shook me to my core. Jack knows how to get meat. Ralph seems to take most of Piggy's insights to heart. Not a wise move there. Piggy is an insolent, immature brat. He has no more knowledge than the bloody monsters that surround me. *Boom!* Jack will probably have fun. Maybe, if I keep a low profile then he won't enslave me. If he tries, he will get a sad wake up call. *Boom, boom, boom!* That is it; I am going to Jack's army. The storm still brews, but, for now, I have decided. Joining Jack is less right than the bloody littluns talking about ghosts! I would do what I wanted from now on. I will be by myself and having an . . . entertaining time. . . .

Here I am, hunting. Who would have thought I would turn into a demon too. I realize now that Jack is the only devil that exists here. This is actually pleasurable. Not in a chuckling way, but in an adrenaline-rushing way. Taking out my wrath on an ugly pig really helps my conscious. I bet *Chief*, meaning Ralph, is just having a jolly good time. Ha! Not really! He must be pining over his missing slaves! Nothing to do but to wish for something that will never be.

—Natalie S., eighth grade

EXCERPT FROM JOURNAL/BLOG ENTRY 4: SIMON SAID

Jack asked us who would join him, more like who would follow. Many raised their hands or shouted in agreement. After we start the "hunt," Roger is the pig and we "attack" him. It mesmerizes me and I feel something wrap around me, grasping my good will and choking it almost to death; I can only hear its diminutive whispers. Something comes out of the shadows and tumbles onto the ground. We run to the beast and start stabbing it; it howls and tries to speak our language. No beast shall live. Every stab I make into it fills me with more power, more energy. I need it; and it's at my disposal ready for my taking. I become more forceful, rain coming down on us; I have to shove the others out of the way to get force behind my thrusts.

A strike of lightning shows the face of the beast. Simon. I have been taking the life out of my friend. I watch him as the last bit of life spouts out of him and gets seeped into the ground. I stumble backwards, falling on to the ground. What have we done? What have I done . . . The one pure person is gone. I stare up into the sky as the thunder rolls on, and the lightning strikes, and the rain never ends. Nothing changes. Death is here, but the world is the same. There is not only rain falling, but tears sliding down my cheeks and under my chin. I curl into a ball and lay looking at the barely visible stars, shivering and knowing I deserve nothing better.

—Sophia K.-L., eighth grade

EXCERPT FROM JOURNAL/BLOG ENTRY 5: RALPH

After his brains splattered over a rock, I made the mistake of throwing my spear into the water next to him. Slowly though, Piggy's body began floating out to the horizon, and my spear had been pushed back to me. So tonight I will search for my spear, which should be at the beach. As I walked down the line of the beach, I began to throw a fit.

"Why is there all of this sand here? It's pathetic. You're pathetic sand!" I yelled, expecting an answer. Nothing came back to me.

"Is that all you do? Just sit here? You're just gonna get blown away by the water!" I looked back at the water. The stars and the full moon shone on the seemingly black water. But it didn't matter cause the stars and the moon are weak.

"One day I'm gonna come up there and beat your guts out!" I yelled to the stars. No answer. I yelled in disgust. I kicked the sand and cursed the stars. I looked across the beach. The various sandy colors that flooded the beach made the green forest seem less threatening. Then, I saw a figure. His hair swooshed up and down like a mop. His brown skin was barely recognizable through the darkness of the night. As he got closer, I prepared myself.

"Whaddaya want ya littlun?" I asked the little boy.

"I have your spear. It was on the shore and I could recognize it from when we met. In the forest," he said with a wry smile. Instantly, images ran around my head as if it felt like they were in a race. The forest, I thought. Then I had remembered the forest. It was my old hunting grounds. I used to hear the dumb birds cry and I'd always look up, but I would never be able to see them because the cloud of leaves always blocked my view. I remembered him, vaguely. By then, the forest scared me somewhat. The creepers hung down like a curtain of monsters and the sliver of light that would be able to creep through the thick trees would be captured by the branches, and then the branches would create a horrifying shadow, similar to the fingers of the devil.

—Tommy H., eighth grade

SAMPLE RESPONSE TO A JOURNAL BLOG ENTRY

Hello, it is me, Thomas Curtis. I read your journal entry and I have a lot of things to say about it. First off, I have to say that I agree about the little ones doing absolutely nothing, although I wouldn't beat them with a vine. I wouldn't do that because it would make me stand out and that would be my death sentence. No offense, but I really would hate to meet your friend Ian. He sounds just dreadful. I hate the talking sort and tend to avoid them. I guess that is because they are about the exact opposite of me. I'd have to agree with you also on the matter of Jack. I don't really know him, but I can tell that he is a wrong sort just by looking into his eyes, his dark power-hungry lustful eyes. I envy your wizard friend Michael from back home. I wish I had a friend like that. Then I wouldn't have to spend all my time sneaking around and I could finally show my face to my enemies, but I could never have that. I am too wary of the fact that anyone can go absolutely wacko and turn on you. I agree with you that the jungle is a cool place, but I am starting to lose my fancy of it little by little. The place is beautiful and I love climbing the trees, but now it seems as though it has a darker side to it. I am going to be outright honest and admit that I am a bit scared of it. I feel as though eyes are trained on me when I am in the jungle, and believe me, that is the last thing I ever want to feel again. I hate it when people take notice of me and watch me, but this is so much worse. I just want to hide in the shadows like I always do. I hope I can trust you though, Watts. I have never revealed my fears to anyone and I don't even know why I am opening up to you.

—William B., eighth grade

Chapter 5

The Point of View Writing Project

My green thumb came only as a result of the mistakes I made while learning to see things from the plant's point of view.

—H. Fred Ale

Overview

This is an integrated social studies/language arts project in which groups of students work collaboratively. Each group creates an historical fiction story, with each member writing the same story from a different character's point of view. The project does not necessarily have to include the historical fiction component, however, and there are easy adaptations presented at the end of the chapter for teachers who would prefer a different theme.

Presented in its entirety, this project presents a high level of academic complexity, similar to what students might expect from a demanding freshman language arts assignment. To be successful, students need to work collaboratively to integrate research about an historical event, location, and time period into their own versions of the story. It is possible to reduce this cognitive demand, and this may be necessary for some students should you implement the project with an entire class.

The project begins with brief activities in which students examine different fairy tales from multiple perspectives. In the next activity, you and another adult each assume the role of the two main characters in a story about a Jewish doctor hiding his family on the property of a Christian baker. One of you tells the story from the doctor's perspective; the other from the baker's. Next, to develop a writing process for the project, students deconstruct the steps a writer might have taken for creating two pieces that are read aloud. These excerpts are from a longer story set at the 1968 Democratic National Convention in Chicago. Students hypothesize the author's research and planning strategies and use these as models for planning their own preparation.

After selecting the historical period in which they wish to place their group's story, students conduct group research and engage in various prewriting activities to develop their storylines. Before drafting, students create character maps to integrate aspects of their research into the characters' background. This is to help them create interesting, historically plausible characters. Finally, students each draft the story from their character's point of view. After peer editing sessions, students share and then submit completed final drafts.

The project takes about 3 weeks if students meet five times a week. It could be done more quickly if you were to reduce the in-class time allotted for research and drafting. It is an ideal project for the final weeks of a school year when even the most dedicated students tend to shift their attention away from academics.

There are several options for grouping students for this project. It could be presented as a small-group enrichment project. You could present it as a whole-class project in which you group strong writers together, and let each group select a time period in which to place their story. Alternatively, you could survey students about their areas of interest and group students with the same preference together. Because it is easy to individualize expectations, you should select the grouping method that best meets your needs.

I first taught this project nearly 20 years ago with Melinda Zibart, a veteran teacher, when we were looking for something motivating and academically challenging for the end of eighth grade. I would like to thank Melinda for her advice in structuring this chapter and for her permission to use the grading system that she developed.

The Cognitive Connection

This project was developed to reinforce the knowledge transformation and problem-solving models of text construction. The knowledge transformation model posits that the writer works on two problems simultaneously, one to create structure and one to determine content. Overriding (i.e., executive) constraints such as "maintain character's personality" and "create a sad mood throughout the story" focus the writer's problem-solving processes on creating a unified text. The more constraints that the writer decides to consider when solving one of the problems, the more cognitively demanding the task becomes.

The writer begins this project with a general sense of the story's structure and a nescient structured body of content—the events of the chosen historical period. The teacher gives the writer some overriding constraints, although these will need to be defined further throughout the writing process. These constraints include the following: maintain a single character's perspective, keep the events and dialogue historically accurate, follow the same storyline as the rest of the group, use figurative language and symbolism when possible, maintain a certain mood, and so forth. As the writing process evolves, these constraints become more articulated and expanded. The writing process is not linear in that the writer will go back and forth among segments of the text as later decisions affect earlier ones. Thus, more successful writers will be engaged in an elaborate writing process. Considering a large number of constraints is the hallmark of good writers—though for many, this never becomes easy. As teachers, we should note that lessening the number of constraints eases the challenge and thus allows us to modify the project for more typical students. This is an option for individualizing this project should you present it to an entire class.

The ill-structured problem-solving model serves as a guide for developing this project. According to this model, intellectual challenge in the problem can come from three places: the problem statement, the criteria for evaluating the final solution, and the path to get from the former to the latter. The more ill-defined these aspects are, the more intellectual effort the problem solver must invest to bring structure to and solve the problem. In this project, all three aspects are left ill-defined for your most talented writers, while you provide the amount of structure needed for the rest of your students. The knowledge transformation model explains how writers make decisions that they consider the correct steps to complete the piece and to solve the problem.

This project also appeals to a variety of intelligences. Although the knowledge transformation model was designed to explain how writers bring language-based projects to fruition, many aspects of the project appeal to other intelligences. Students with an interpersonal strength can focus on the characters' emotional responses. Students with a visual strength can include art to complement the story. Students with an intrapersonal strength can focus on the relationships among characters. One should note that learning-styles-based instruction has come under some criticism lately (see Stansbury, 2010, for a discussion). However, for this project, it remains relevant.

National Standards

FROM THE INTERNATIONAL READING ASSOCIATION AND NATIONAL COUNCIL OF TEACHERS OF ENGLISH (1996):
- Students employ a wide range of strategies as they write and use different writing process elements appropriately to communicate with different audiences for a variety of purposes.

- Students apply knowledge of language structure, language conventions (e.g., spelling and punctuation), media techniques, figurative language, and genre to create, critique, and discuss print and nonprint texts.

- Students conduct research on issues and interests by generating ideas and questions, and by posing problems. They gather, evaluate, and synthesize data from a variety of sources (e.g., print and nonprint texts, artifacts, people) to communicate their discoveries in ways that suit their purpose and audience.

- Students use a variety of technological and information resources (e.g., libraries, databases, computer networks, video) to gather and synthesize information and to create and communicate knowledge.

- Students develop an understanding of and respect for diversity in language use, patterns, and dialects across cultures, ethnic groups, geographic regions, and social roles.

OBJECTIVES

Students will:

1. Rewrite a classic fairy tale from two different characters' points of view.
2. Research an historical period in 20th-century American history and integrate this research into their writing.
3. Work cooperatively to write an historical fiction piece, each group member writing the story from a different character's viewpoint.
4. Develop a multidimensional character.
5. Create a mood through setting, language, and plot.
6. Create illustrations that enhance the mood of the story.
7. Present the story through a variety of formats.

Lesson 1: Introducing the Project

PROCEDURE

1. **Explain** that students are going to work in small groups to write an historical fiction piece. Each group member will write the same story, but from a different character's point of view.

2. **Ask** what "point of view" means. (Encourage students to go beyond definitions of first, second, and third person to explain that point of view can also include the person through whose eyes we see and come to understand the story. This means that the narrator is not an unspecified person but rather a character who may be involved in the actions, who is not objective, and who may or may not be telling the whole truth.)

3. **Show students** a picture of the interior of an English car in which the steering wheel is on the right. (You should be able to find a good example by searching Google images for "English automobile interior" or "English Jaguar interior.") Ask the following questions to elicit the idea that there is not a correct side for the steering wheel, but that the preferred location depends on a person's point of view:

   - Is anything wrong with this picture—particularly the steering wheel?
   - If you were to show a similar picture of the interior of an American car, what might English students say about the steering wheel being on the left?
   - On which side does the steering wheel belong?

4. **Explain** that different points of view do not necessarily mean that one person is right and the other is wrong, but that different people interpret the same events differently. Ask how the three bears might tell the story of coming home and finding a stranger sleeping in their house.

5. **Explain** that in the first assignment, students are to imagine that a trial has occurred based on events in a fairy tale. Their assignment is to write both closing arguments—the defendant's and the prosecutor's. Read the following example, written by a seventh grader, aloud to the class. Ask your students to imagine that they are members of the jury.

Closing Arguments in the Trial of Hansel and Gretel v. Their Father: A Petition for Child Emancipation

FOR THE PROSECUTION

As Hansel and Gretel's lawyer in this case, I would like to say that these children are better off alone. They do not need their father taking care of them, if he is even capable of that. The last time Hansel and Gretel were left in the hands of their father, he sent them away into the forest twice the second things got difficult. They had no provisions. They could have starved. Chances are another chance at parenting is too much for him; he'll send them away again, maybe even to their deaths this time. Hansel and Gretel's father's main idea in his final argument was that they were too young to take care of themselves; that they needed him to help them. Last time I checked, Hansel outwitted his father and his stepmother the first time they sent him and Gretel away, proving that he was smarter than either of them! The second time they sent them away, Gretel was smart enough to save her brother from being eaten by the witch they encountered. They were able to keep themselves alive. Hansel and Gretel are most definitely smart enough to be living on their own and free from their father. People say that children need their father, but this family right here is the exception. These children do not need their father; all they need is each other. The truth is, all that children need is love, and Hansel and Gretel's father does not love them. They do not need him. These two children will be able to go on with their lives happily if you choose to emancipate them today. If they are forced to stay connected with their father, who knows what their lives will be like. In some cases, a child needs a parent, but in this case all these children need is to be loved, and not by their father, but by each other. Emancipating these children today means they will be able to live together happily, without having to see or talk to their horrible father.

Thank you.

FOR THE DEFENSE

As Hansel and Gretel's father's representation in this case, I would like to make it clear that Hansel and Gretel are still very young; much too young to become emancipated and live by themselves. There is no way that they would be able to keep themselves fed and healthy, let alone run a household! Now I know my client made some decisions that many people see as parenting mistakes in the past, but haven't we all? My client's choices were all completely logical. If he hadn't brought Hansel and Gretel into the forest those two times, his horrible ex-wife would have abused them and deprived them of food and water. Their home life would have been much more dangerous than their life in the forest. My client had his children's best interest in mind. He knew there was food to be found in the forest and that his children would be safe for a short time. He is a great father and his children need him. All children need their father, and a father needs his children. My client has recognized that being with his ex-wife was dangerous and a huge mistake. He is now focused on being the best father to his kids as he possibly can be. To take his kids away from him and emancipate them would be horrible for their family, or what is left of it. We can't ruin this small family's lives together. These kids need their father to be there for them for their entire lives, not just a fragment of it. My client will be able to make every meal, drive everywhere, and keep up the household while his children go on with their school work and the rest of their lives. If they were emancipated, they would be forced to deal with the stress of a child's life and a parent's life. These kids cannot survive without their father. Their father is perfectly capable of taking care of them and they should not be emancipated and trusted to take care of themselves. Let my client show what he is truly capable of; give him his children and let this family live happily ever after.

—Bryna C., seventh grader

1. **Ask** students the following questions about these closing arguments:
   - What were the agreed-upon facts in both closing arguments? (Hansel and Gretel were sent into the woods twice by their father. They had no food.)
   - Which side gave the more compelling argument? Is either side wrong? (Discuss several answers, but stress that right or wrong depends on point of view.)
   - What might you have added or said differently? (Discuss several answers.)
   - Would you vote to emancipate the children? (Take a vote count.)

2. **Ask** students to think of other fairy tales that might be seen differently if told from another character's point of view (e.g., the three little pigs from the wolf's perspective might become the story of three bad neighbors). List these in a place that all students can see from their desks.

HOMEWORK

Students should complete the following:

Select one of the fairy tales from the list brainstormed above, define charges one character could bring against another (e.g., the three bears could charge Goldilocks with trespassing), and write the closing arguments for lawyers on both sides of the case.

Lesson 2: Starting the Story

PROCEDURE

1. **Have** several children read their closing arguments to the class. Use the discussion question about the Hansel and Gretel closing arguments from the previous lesson to discuss the pieces that were read aloud. Collect and grade the homework, if you wish.

2. **Explain** the following:
   - There are often several points of view in a story, and the stories they are going to write are going to be based on real-life historical (or current) events.
   - Students are going to work in partners or small groups to write a story that takes place during a significant event in 20th-century American history. (Limit the time range to what works best for your class. I would avoid eras with which they are not familiar or that they have not studied in a recent history class.)
   - Within a group, the different stories need not follow identical time-lines and the characters do not have to interact throughout the story. Rather, the main characters in each one need to come together at a key moment and impact each other.
   - Students are going to hear a story told from two characters' points of view. They should listen for agreed-upon events, references that place the story in the actual event, and how each character sees the same events differently.

For this introductory activity, you will either need another teacher to tell the story with you, or you may have two students prepare it in advance. Each person should tell the store from his or her point of view in first person. Explain that you are each role-playing a person who might have lived in Amsterdam during the Nazi invasion of 1940: one a Jewish doctor, the other a Christian baker. This story is about how their lives came together. (Note that the second piece is written for a female character, but it can easily be adapted to a male.)

CHARACTER 1: A JEWISH DOCTOR

Becoming a doctor had been one of the few professions available to a Jewish student in Austria in the 1930s. After graduation, I did a fellowship at a public clinic in Amsterdam where I met my wife, a nurse. We lived in a small apartment on a canal in the Jewish section of town. Soon after the Germans declared war in 1939, the Dutch declared themselves a neutral nation, and although we heard stories about horrors in Eastern Europe, we lived in relative peace—for a little while. The Nazis invaded in May of 1940 and everything changed that winter. In February, the Germans began deporting Jews, and the Dutch people organized a protest strike. The leaders of the strike were killed. A Nazi officer came to the clinic and told another doctor to serve on a Jewish council—a Judenrat. When he said that he refused, the officer immediately shot him in the head. My friend fell to the floor, eyes wide open, blood pouring out the wound. The Nazi grabbed a towel from a table, threw it at me, and had me wipe the blood off the floor. He turned and left. Still holding the blood-soaked towel, I ran and found my wife. We had heard about Jews hiding in store rooms at the zoo, but had no idea who to contact—who to trust. A gentile woman, a patient, who I had saved in a difficult surgery, had been at the clinic for a checkup when this happened. She slipped me a piece of paper with an address on it. It also read, "come tonight." In a panic, my wife and I gathered all the money we could—we didn't have much—and one suitcase and went to the address—a shabby house by any standard on the outskirts of Amsterdam. The woman was a saint. At great risk to herself, she took us immediately to her sister's house somewhere in Amsterdam. We didn't know where because we were hidden under boxes in the back of a small truck. The woman's sister owned a bakery that had a tiny basement—dirt floor, no windows, you couldn't stand up. We were safe—or so we thought. For 2 months we hid in that crawl space of a room, paying her money every week. Then, without warning, she told us we had to leave. She said it was too dangerous to hide Jews, that Germans were searching houses. We had recently given her the last of our money, which she conveniently said she had spent on black market food for us. I didn't believe her—after all, she owned a bakery. I reminded her about saving her sister's life. She said we had to leave immediately because she couldn't risk her life. She had her own family.

CHARACTER 2: A CHRISTIAN BAKER

I love my sister. I know he saved her life. But what was I to do? My sister's husband had been forced to work in a German factory that had been bombed by the allies—simply because he would not join the German army. I know I owned a bakery. But the Germans routinely took food out of the Netherlands and kept the entire population on limited rations. Imagine what it was like to see my own children hungry. But still I kept them hidden. Now there was a group of Dutch collaborators who were making money by finding and turning in hidden Jews. It was only a matter of time before they searched my house. Buying food on the black market had been difficult because I didn't want to raise suspicion; it got more and more risky and more and more expensive. The price for being caught with Jews in the house was death to the family that hid them. I had children. He was a doctor and he should have understood.

3. **Ask** students to identify the large historical event and the specific part of that event in which the story is placed. (WWII is the larger event, and the German invasion of Amsterdam is the specific part of the war in which the story takes place.)

4. **Use** the following questions to discuss the piece:
   - Were there other specific historical events within the story? (the deportation of Dutch Jews; the forming of the Jewish Council; the hiding of Jews and the search for them; the rationing of food in the Netherlands)
   - Were there any particular details or language that gave the piece authenticity? (Discuss several answers, such as the hiding of Jews in the zoo, the forced employment of the Dutch, the word "Judenrat" used for the name of the council.)
   - Is either person wrong? What would you tell the baker to do? (Discuss several answers.)
   - From who else's point of view could this story be told? (the doctor's wife, the baker's sister, the baker's child, a Dutch citizen who searched for and turned in Dutch Jews who were in hiding)

(If you are having students write about current events, skip the next activity.)

5. **Select** a central place where everyone can see what is being written. List the decades or time periods from which students are allowed to select their events.

6. **Elicit** from students a list of significant events about which they may want to write that occurred during the listed time periods (e.g., the Great Depression, World War II, the Vietnam War). Have students go to the board and list the events under the decades during which they took place.

7. **Assign** groups or allow students a few minutes to select their own small groups. (When choosing the latter option, I don't allow more than four students to a group. I also encourage more talented writers to work together.)

8. **Allow** time for group members to select a general event from the list and then to decide upon two specific historical events that occurred in this larger context. Encourage students to decide upon a limited time period in selecting their specific events as this will allow for a more effective story. Using the introductory story as an example, the author selected the hiding of Jewish citizens after the Nazi invasion of the Netherlands—not the entire invasion, and definitely not WWII.)

9. **Have** each group share its choices and guide students to select the better of the two based upon the following criteria:
   - Are there distinct perspectives from which the event may be told?
   - Is the event specific enough that the story may be told in four (or whatever number you decide) pages?
   - Does it seem realistic that groups can find the needed historical materials during the few days allotted for research?
   - Is there a strong conflict to drive the story?

10. **Approve** the final topic for each group according to these guidelines.

HOMEWORK

Students should complete the following:

Write a one-page summary of the event that your group has chosen. Use at least two sources; be sure to properly cite the sources at the end of your piece.

Lesson 3: Deconstructing a Sample

PROCEDURE

1. **Have** students meet in groups and read their summaries aloud. Have group members write a composite summary and complete Handout 1: Group Plot Summary (found at the end of this chapter). Collect and grade the homework and the completed handout, if you wish.

2. **Have** students meet in their groups for 5 minutes to brainstorm things they will need to know before they can begin writing. Explain that these may be significant aspects of the event, such as the location of a particular battle, or they may be minor details, such as what was the cost of a stamp at the time of the event. While in groups, they also should brainstorm a list of characters from whose perspective their story can be told. Characters do not need to have opposing points of view, but there needs to be significant differences among them to make each story unique.

3. **Explain** to students that before they begin researching their stories, they are going to *deconstruct* a writing sample. Explain that in literature, deconstructing a piece of writing means analyzing it by breaking it down into its component parts. Today, they are also going to analyze the research process in which the author engaged that proved the information needed to give both pieces historical authenticity. To do this, they are going to listen to each piece in its entirety and then reread it paragraph by paragraph as they deconstruct it.

4. **Read** the following introduction to the model story so that students have a context: The late 1960s was a contentious time in America. Many groups of people had strong, and often conflicting, attitudes towards the United States' continued involvement in the Vietnam War. The tension between these groups was exacerbated by conflicting views over the draft—a national program that required all male citizens, upon turning 18, to register with the government. Soon after registering, many of these Americans were called to serve in the military. This conflict between opposing groups gave rise to the growing counter-culture—or hippie—movement that seemed to reject the values of many older Americans. The conflict came to a head at the 1968 Democratic Convention that was held in Chicago, IL.

5. **Tell** students that as they are listening to you read, they should to try to imagine what information the author had to know before beginning to write. Read the following excerpts aloud.

Festival of Life: A Story About the 1968 Democratic National Convention

EXCERPT 1: FROM THE HIPPIE'S POINT OF VIEW

(1) It was August 28th, 1968. I had just left the movie theater, having seen "Planet of the Apes" for the second time. A great movie, and although everyone I knew who had seen it had said they had predicted the "surprise ending," I had not. A policeman was leaving the movie at the same time I was. He barely looked old enough to be in uniform. His hair was kind of long—for a cop—but kind of short compared to mine. For some reason, he stopped to talk when we got to the door at the same time. "Oh, great," I thought. "Getting hassled by 'the man.' And for what?" He asked, "You see that ending coming?' Well, that wasn't what I was expecting. I was so thrown by his question that I didn't really know what to say and just looked at him for a second. "Umm, yeah. But I saw it before. Still worth the buck fifty." He sort of smiled—but looked more confused—like he never really expected an actual reply. Cops.

(2) I flashed him a peace sign that he didn't see. "Hey, peace," I called. He turned around. "Yeah, peace." Cops. Go figure. He headed south. And I walked east toward Grant Park. I had heard thousands of hippies, YIPpies, and other groovy people had gathered there to protest "the man"—a protest of the Vietnam War that had forced President Johnson to not run for reelection. But it looked like Humphrey—his vice-president—was going to run instead. Different suit. Same ideas. Was there any point to voting? The energy as I got closer to the park was amazing, and I knew it was going to be what I expected. The Summer of Love finally made its way to Chicago. A big party—if I could get past the security. The streets were full of flower children and cops—and people who looked liked cops—nobody in between.

(3) In my backpack were about 25 belts that I had made from strips of red and blue striped burlap that I had bought at Marshall Fields in the upholstery section. I had planned to sell them for a buck each. OK, they weren't fringed vests, but they were groovy man, groovy. From what I heard on VW radio, I thought that I knew what to expect, but I didn't. A wall of police and National Guard members on Michigan Avenue; across the street, in Grant Park, a sea of teenagers. No one seemed over 30. Good. I found a small space under an American flag and set up shop. A guy with a yellow T-shirt emblazoned with a big red peace sign was using a bull horn to give a speech. He looked like John Lennon and was hard to hear over the crowd. A lot of people were listening, but a lot more were making music—several with green tambourines—like the song. Maybe I'd trade some of my belts for one.

(4) The mood changed in a second. A young guy pulled down the flag and—boom—the police were on him. All I could see was a circle of cops around him—like a football huddle. It looked like they were beating him. And for what? I was furious and scared. Getting caught up in the moment, I bent down to pick up a rock. As I stood, a cop with a billy club in his raised hand was standing over me. It was the cop from the movie.

EXCERPT 2: FROM THE POLICEMAN'S POINT OF VIEW

(1) I had only been on the Chicago police force for a little while and had been assigned to the first district, downtown. This meant a lot to me because my father had been a sergeant at that district, before he was shot while trying to stop a robbery in progress and had gone on permanent disability. I was a third-generation Irish cop and proud of it. I had just gotten engaged and had my eye on a bungalow in Bridgeport, the neighborhood where I had grown up. It had a nice yard that would be perfect for kids. Now, if I could just get through the Democratic Convention this week, everything would be perfect. I sort of felt bad for President Johnson having to decide that he wouldn't run again, but I liked his vice-president Hubert Humphrey now that he had come out in support of the Vietnam War. I thought all of the hippies were wrong to be so opposed to the war. I mean, what did they think would happen to the world if the Communists won? But free speech and different opinions are part of what makes this country great and something that the communists didn't allow.

(2) I had gone to the early movie because I wanted to be sure I was downtown for my shift which started at 3:00 and ended at 11:00. Like every cop in Chicago, I was on high alert, wanting to support the mayor who had been so good to us—having given us raises and all. So I went to see Planet of the Apes. It was a great movie with a surprise ending. I wondered if the hippies would get the message. As I was leaving, I saw one and wanted to talk to him about it. So I asked him if he was surprised by the final scene. He looked at me like he was expecting me to arrest him. He just stood there stunned, before answering. He seemed like a nice guy, even though he needed a haircut. I walked south on State Street to the police station at 11th. It was a perfect Wednesday afternoon. I mean, at least the weather was perfect. The streets were crowded with hippies who glared at me and normal-looking people who smiled. It seemed as if everyone had chosen sides. I wish it hadn't been like that.

(3) After role call, a group of us were marched to Michigan Avenue where we were to keep the kids in the park separated from the hotels where a lot of conventioneers were staying. We had been warned that the YIPpies were going to cause trouble. I was told to stand on the park side of the street. I hoped nothing bad would happen. But the sheer numbers in the park spelled trouble. I guess I was little jumpy. Then it all took place so fast. I

> saw a flag get lowered and a bunch of cops and I charged in. I never knew the details and it didn't really matter. The kids instantly went nuts and surrounded the cops like a tidal wave. All I wanted to do was keep them separate from a small group of officers in the middle of the crowd. I saw a kid bend down to pick up a rock; I knew what he was going to do with it. Acting on instinct, I raised my billy club behind him. But when he stood up, it was the kid from the movie.

6. **Ask** students if they have any initial reactions to the two excerpts. (Discuss several answers.)

7. **Ask** students the following questions about the piece as a whole:
   - What is the particular large historical event in which the story takes place? (The 1968 Democratic National Convention)
   - What part of this event does the story focus on? (The fight between the police and the protesters in Grant Park.)
   - How did each character see the final event? (The hippie saw the police charging into attack a boy who didn't deserve it. The cop saw it as a group of hippies attacking his fellow officers.)

8. **Distribute** copies of Handout 2: Point of View Grading Sheet (found at the end of this chapter). Explain that this sheet lists the criteria upon which students will be graded. Review each criterion. Ask students to assume that they are the teacher. Explain that each story is a small selection from the larger piece and ask students to use these criteria as the basis for a letter grade for each excerpt. Discuss what grade students feel each piece deserves.

9. **Explain** that students are going to discuss each paragraph to see what kind of preparation and research the writer needed to do to give the piece an authentic feel of Chicago in the 1960s.

10. **Assign** each student one of the paragraphs from the excerpt. As you reread the piece, say the numbers that precede each topic sentence. Have students strive to list three to five historical references that are in their assigned paragraphs. Remind students that the references may include major events or something as simple as the use of slang indicative of the time. If a reference appears in both stories, it is OK to note it a second time.

PARAGRAPH 1
- *Planet of the Apes* was a popular movie in the summer of 1968.
- Hair length was a reflection of political and personal philosophy.
- Movies cost $1.50.

PARAGRAPH 2
- Peace signs were a hippie symbol.
- "Peace" was a hippie greeting with political, antiwar implications.

- Hippies were young people who tended to be anti-establishment. YIPpies were a political subgroup. Being a YIPpie meant that you belonged to the Youth International Party.
- "Groovy" was slang, much as "cool" is now.
- "The man" was slang for a person in the mainstream culture with established power.
- Johnson did not run for reelection because of the controversy over the Vietnam War.
- Hubert Humphrey, his vice president, was one of several Democratic candidates for president. Shortly before the convention, he made a statement supporting the war.
- "Summer of Love" was an unprecedented gathering of hippies in San Francisco in 1967.
- "Flower children" was an alternative name for hippies.

PARAGRAPH 3

- Marshall Fields was a large department store chain in Chicago throughout the 1960s. The downtown store had an upholstery department.
- A fringed vest was a piece of hippie clothing.
- VW stands for Volkswagen. It was an inexpensive, small car popular with hippies.
- There were many police and National Guard members protecting the streets in Chicago during the convention.
- Michigan Avenue is a downtown Chicago street that separates large buildings on the west side from Grant park on the east.
- Grant Park is a very large park in downtown Chicago where the hippies tried to stay during their protest.
- T-shirts with peace signs were popular hippie clothing.
- John Lennon was a member of the Beatles.
- *Green Tambourine* was a popular song of the time.

PARAGRAPH 4

- A young boy pulled down a flag.
- The flag lowering ignited the police charge into the park.
- Hippies threw things at the police.
- Police used billy clubs.

PARAGRAPH 5

- The downtown police district was the first district.
- There is a neighborhood in Chicago called Bridgeport. It has houses designed in the bungalow style.
- President Johnson was not running for reelection.
- Hubert Humphrey supported the Vietnam War.

- The United States opposed the Communists during the war.

PARAGRAPH 6
- Police shifts ran from 3 p.m. to 11 p.m.
- The mayor had recently given the police raises.
- *Planet of the Apes* was a popular movie in the summer of 1968.
- The police station was located at 11th and State.
- August 28th was a Wednesday. The weather was good.

PARAGRAPH 7
- Grant Park was within walking distance of the police station.
- YIPpies were a political subgroup of the hippie movement. Being a YIPpie meant that you belonged to the Youth International Party.
- There were a large number of hippies in the park.
- The flag lowering ignited the police charge into the park.
- Hippies threw things at the police.
- Police used billy clubs.

11. **Select** a central place where many students can write and everyone can see what is being written. Have a representative from each group go to the board and rewrite the group's list large enough for everyone to read.
12. **Give** each group 5 minutes to generate four or five categories into which all the listed items could be separated. Should you need an example of a possible category, ask the class which of the listed items could be placed into a category entitled "Slang and Words of the Time" (groovy, the man, flower child, hippie, YIPpie).
13. **Have** each group select a representative to share the group's list of categories. Have the class agree upon a final set. Explain that this set of category titles is the set that each group will research so that students will be able to create an authentic mood for the time and setting of their stories. A good set of categories might include the following:
    - Facts about the larger event
    - Facts about the specific event
    - Facts about location at the time of the event
    - Pop culture (e.g., language and slang, prices, clothing, music)
    - Important things we need to know

14. **Distribute** Handout 3: Research Sites (found at the end of this chapter). Explain that students will need this handout to complete the homework.

HOMEWORK
Students should complete the following:

For each research category, list two facts that characterize the era or event that is central to your story. Use the websites on the handout as a starting point, but you also may use other sites that you find. Be sure to create a bibliography of all of the sites from which you select items.

Lesson 4: Research

PROCEDURE

1. **Have** students share their homework within their groups. Have each group select a few facts to share with the entire class.

2. **Explain** that students will each need to have a brief summary of each character's story before beginning their research. This summary should be considered tentative as it might evolve as students gather their research.

3. **Ask** a few students to extemporaneously offer a brief summary that the author of the sample excerpts might have used. (On August 28th, 1968, in Chicago, a hippie goes to a movie where he had a chance discussion with a policeman about its surprise ending. He then goes to Grant Park where a crowd has gathered to protest the Democratic National Convention that is in town. A fight between the protesters and police break out. The hippie is about to become involved when he comes face to face with the policeman he met at the movie.)

4. **Have** the groups each write a plot summary for a story from which all members can draw their own individual character's story. Then have each group member write a paragraph version of this story from her or his character's point of view. Reiterate that the different stories need not follow identical timelines and that the characters do not have to interact throughout each story. Rather, the main characters in each one need to come together at a key moment and impact each other. (You might want to circulate among the groups during this session to offer advice on students' plot lines.)

5. **Have** each group share its general summary with the class. Class members should respond with suggestions for research (e.g., What movie did he see? How many people attended the protest?).

6. **Have** groups generate a list of questions for each of the categories that they have decided to research. Explain that this is a starting point and the list of questions should expand and change as students conduct their research. Have each group decide on a research strategy (e.g., each person will research a different question; each person will research the time period first and then the group will decide specific research assignments).

7. **Allow** students time to begin researching.

HOMEWORK

Students should complete the following:

Find 10 facts that might possibly become details in your group's stories. Each student also should write a research plan for the next two class periods by listing the kinds of research they will conduct over the next few days.

Note to teachers: You may wish to make advanced plans with the school or community librarian to pull materials for the students or to conduct a lesson on bibliography citations. Research options for the plans may include, but should not be limited to, the following:

- Work with the school librarian to find books on the event or the decade.
- Arrange interviews with staff members who lived during the time in which you are writing.
- Arrange live, telephone, or online interviews with grandparents, parents, and acquaintances who lived through the time period or who experienced the event.
- Write interview questions in advance of any interviews.
- Continue with online research.
- Search online photo galleries such as the American Memories Collection at the Library of Congress (http://memory.loc.gov/ammem/browse). This collection may be searched by topic, decade, or type of materials and has a link to the photo collection.

Lesson 5: Continuing the Research

PROCEDURE

1. **Have** several students share their research plans and the specific steps that they will follow to bring the plans to fruition. (This might raise new research options for other groups that they had not previously considered.)

2. **Have** students keep a record of the resources that they use, adding to the list each time a new one is used. (If necessary, review the citation formatting that you require or teach students to use EasyBib [http://www.easybib.com], a free online bibliography maker.)

3. **Allow** two or three class periods for research. Begin each class by having students share their research plans for the day. If you wish, collect and grade the research.

HOMEWORK

Students should complete the following over the next few nights:

- Write summaries of your research.
- Update a bibliography.
- List facts under the appropriate category from the list developed in Lesson 3.
- Prepare a research plan for the following day.

Lesson 6: Character Maps and Drafting

PROCEDURE

1. **Explain** to students that even though the characters in companion stories do not need to participate in all of the same events, the references to the things they have in common must match. For example, if two characters meet at a movie, one cannot have seen *Planet of the Apes* while the other has seen *The Green Berets,* even if both films were popular at the same time. If students use more generic references, they still must match in companion pieces. If, for example, a character drives to a destination in one person's story, she cannot take a bus in another.

2. **Have** students meet to integrate their group research into their summaries. They should go through the group summary event by event and add as many period and event-specific details to each event as possible. Tell them to agree upon details, such as what happens at what time in the story, how people get from event to event, what they see in their surroundings, and so forth.

3. **Tell** students that before they begin writing, they should have a clear sense of their main character's personality. Reread aloud the first two paragraphs of the hippie's story. Use the following questions to discuss the character:
   - What are his initial attitudes toward the policeman? How are these revealed? (He is suspicious of him. This is seen in his response to the officer's approach after the movie when he assumes it will be a negative experience. He refers to the officer as "the man"; this is a negative term used at the time of the piece to refer to authority figures.)
   - What surprised him about the officer? (The officer's longer than usual hair surprises him as it goes against his preconceived notions. Moreover, he is surprised by the officer's response to the "peace" greeting.)
   - Why might the author have included these details about the officer? (It gives the policeman some dimension as a character. It challenges the hippie's preconceptions.)
   - Why does he go to the park? Is it for political reasons? (He goes because he expects a party atmosphere, not to participate in the protest. He seems to want to be part of the experience of being there.)
   - How does the author reveal the hippie's level of political concern without using summary statements such as, "I wasn't very political"? (He shows the reader the hippie's politics by telling his general understanding for the events that caused the protest and then having the character focus on the party atmosphere.)

4. **Explain** that establishing and maintaining a strong, distinctive personality for the main character is an important goal for writers. Otherwise, the pieces will not have an understandable point of view. The research should

help them not only detail the event, but also give them information such as characteristic language and clothing that they can use to establish the character's personality within the historical context.

5. **Reread** aloud the first two paragraphs of the policeman's story. Have students meet in groups to list ways in which the author reveals the character's personality and politics without using such words as "conservative" or "traditional" that tell what they are. Have a spokesperson from each group share the group's conclusions (e.g., The character is proud of his family's tradition of joining the Chicago Police Department. He has traditional values, embracing such things as getting married, buying a house, and having children. He also seems to have empathy for President Johnson and although he disagrees with the antiwar view, he has respect for opinions other than his own. This respect for people not like him is revealed again in the second paragraph when he calls the hippie a "nice guy" even though the hippie's haircut was not in keeping with his own values.)

6. **Explain** that, before students begin drafting, they need a strong sense of the main character's personality. To articulate this personality, they should create a bubble map of the character according to the following directions. Explain that all of the samples you are going to give describe the police officer.

- At the top of a piece of paper, make a circle. In the circle, write the character's full name and a few short phrases that detail her or his personality (e.g., police officer, traditional values, fair minded).

- Extending from this circle, draw four lines. At the end of each of these, make other circles. Label the first one "Character Details." Draw at least four circles extending from this one. Write a key detail about the character in each one (e.g., 24 years old, 6' 1", 190 pounds, engaged to high school sweetheart, planning to be married on Christmas day).

- In a second circle, write "Favorite Things." Draw at least four circles extending from this one. Write something special that the character likes in each one (e.g., favorite movie: can't decide between *The Green Berets*, a pro-Vietnam War movie, and *Planet of the Apes*, a science fiction story; favorite actor: John Wayne; favorite food: McDonald's hamburgers; favorite sports team: Chicago White Sox, from the south side of the city).

- In a third circle, write "Important Things He Has." Draw at least four circles extending from this one. Write something the character values in each one (e.g., Purple Heart from when he was injured in Vietnam; picture taken with his father and grandfather the day he graduated from the police academy; letterman's sweater from high school; trophy from high school debate team).

- In a third circle, write "Job and Hobbies." Draw at least four circles extending from this one. Write a detail about the character's school, career, or interests in each one (e.g., just graduated from the police academy; works out at the local YMCA three times a week; writes his grandmother once a week; has a dog that he found in an alley; joined the army after graduating high school).

- In a Fourth Circle, write "Other." Draw at least four circles extending from this one. Write an interesting detail about the character in each one. Try to use this section of the bubble map to give the character some dimension, but keep the details believable (e.g., still friends with high school buddy who became a hippie; misses *The Andy Griffith Show*—a comedy about a small-town sheriff—that was recently canceled; liked President Kennedy a lot; likes The Beatles).

7. **Allow** students time to create bubble maps for their main characters. Explain that many of the details should be consistent with the personality description in the first bubble.

8. **Have** students meet in groups of three or four (not necessarily their writing groups). They should read aloud the bubble map to the group, but not say the personality traits that are written in the main bubble. After a student has finished reading, have other group members try to guess the personality traits that the reader was trying to show. If the other members cannot guess the trait, they should offer suggestions that would make the key trait more evident. (To begin this activity, you may want to have a few students share their maps with the entire class so that you can model the discussion.)

9. **Have** groups decide an interesting title for their collective set of stories.

10. **Review** a timeline for their writing (e.g., three days to draft, one day to edit, one day to share final versions).

11. **Have** students begin drafting their stories. Remind them to begin with the group title and a title for their individual piece. Throughout their individual stories, they should strive to reveal something about the historical period and about the character's personality in each paragraph. Furthermore, if they are unsure about an historical detail, they should be intentionally vague. As an example of this situation, explain that in the sample pieces, the author wasn't sure about the name of a movie theatre that existed in Chicago's downtown area in 1968, so there was no mention of the theatre in which the characters saw the movie.

HOMEWORK

Students should complete the following:

Complete the first page of your stories.

Lesson 7: Finishing the Drafts

Repeat this lesson until the drafts are completed.

PROCEDURE

1. **Have** students meet in their writing groups to share their first pages. Group members should discuss the following:
   - Are all of the stories within the group consistent in terms of plot, characters mentioned (e.g., if a character is alone in one story, she can't be with a friend in another), and historical references?
   - Are all historical references consistent?
   - Has each writer revealed the main character's personality and included historical references in each paragraph?

2. **Have** students continue to draft the next segment of the story.

HOMEWORK

Students should complete the following:

   Complete another section of your story.

Lesson 8: Peer Editing

PROCEDURE

1. **Have** students exchange completed drafts. Have them correct each other's drafts for consistency with the group summary. (The dialogue does not need to match perfectly.) Editors also should comment on other story aspects, such as point of view, character, grammar, and setting as detailed on Handout 2: Point of View Grading Sheet.

HOMEWORK

Students should complete the following:

Complete the final versions of your story.

Lesson 9: Final Sharing

PROCEDURE

1. **Have** students select a favorite passage from their stories.
2. **Have** students come to the front of the room in groups and share their selected passages.
3. **Have** other students comment on what they thought each author or group did particularly well.
4. **Collect and grade** final stories.

Challenging Minds: Highlighted Activities

Following is a list of activities used in this unit that can be adapted to many instructional and enrichment situations to complement a variety of student strengths.

1. **Student graders:** In grades 5–8, I often have students grade sample writings. These are usually samples that I have created. I have students assume the role of teacher, grade the sample, and write comments on what was well done and what might be improved. Often, I give two samples for the same assignment: one that is well-written and one that is flawed. Students always seem to like assuming the role of teacher. Moreover, I find it gives me a great deal of insight into both their own writing process and their understanding of what would be expected from the assignment at hand.

2. **Character maps:** It is my personal bias that if you want students to become effective writers, character is as important as plot in driving a story. If students have a strong sense of a character's personality and motivation, then they should know how that character would respond in any situation. Furthermore, as part of the knowledge transformation process, the character's personality serves as an overriding constraint that shapes the writer's decisions on a story's structure and content. I like having a young author place the character's key personality trait in the central bubble and having all other bubbles reflect this trait. As a check, I have students share the content of secondary and tertiary bubbles and then have other students try to figure out the trait that the author was trying to show. Often, this checking process helps students realize that there is a consistency among the details and that the map needs editing to create this consistency. With a completed character map, students have a concrete guide to making decisions about many character-related details in their story.

Adaptations

1. If you prefer, the focus of the assignment does not have to be 20th-century American historical fiction. One alternative could be current events, such as a fire in California or a recent election. Students also could focus on social-emotional issues, such as bullying or being new to a school. Should you use this latter option, I suggest that, as part of the project, you have students read *Games: A Tale of Two Bullies*, a novel by Carol Gorman. This novel is written from the alternating perspectives of the two main characters who take turns telling parts of a single story. It is, however, a good example of how point of view affects a person's interpretation of events and people.

2. Add other story elements to the focus. Depending on the grade level at which I taught this lesson and the strengths of the writers with whom I worked, I would increase the number of literary elements that I expect that writers should incorporate into their stories. For example, I might have students spend time developing a setting in much the same way they detailed how they developed the character. I would then discuss how setting, character, and literary devices such as metaphor and symbolism combine to create mood. Adding these elements to the requirements would be a good way to adapt the assignment for stronger writers should you present this project to an entire class.

3. Ask students to include historically and regionally appropriate metaphorical language. For example, should they write about desegregation of schools in the 20th century, an appropriate simile might be, "She was from the North, but she was as pretty as a magnolia blossom." Or, if the story were set in the Great Depression, "he was about as dependable as a rebuilt starter on a Model T Ford" might add to the mood of the piece.

4. Have students include illustrations. These could include drawings or photographs. Suggest that, for some pictures, students might take snapshots of hands holding important objects, or dress up in period clothing. Students also could find copyright-free pictures on the Internet that might reflect a mood in their piece.

5. Have the students record their stories as books on CDs.

Name: _____ Date: _____

Handout 1
Group Plot Summary

Group members:

General historical event:

Specific historical event (occurring within the larger event):

Specific range of dates in which your story occurs:

Location of your story:

Names, ages, gender, occupation, and key personality trait(s) of each main character:

Attach a one-paragraph summary of your group's story. Include the central problem and its resolution in your summary.

Name: _____ Date: _____

Handout 2
Point of View Grading Sheet

As you begin writing your individual historical fiction story, be sure to follow these guidelines **very carefully** to ensure that you receive maximum credit for this assignment. Make sure that your individual story is consistent with your group's plot summary, your individual summary, and your group members' stories.

POINT OF VIEW
_____/5   Story is told in a consistent point of view: first or third person
_____/5   Story is consistent with approved plot summary
_____/15   Story correlates with companion piece(s) by other group members

MAIN CHARACTER
_____/5   Character's full name and age are stated in text
_____/10   Character's external conflict is clear
_____/10   Character's external resolution is clear
_____/10   Character's internal conflict is clear
_____/10   Character's internal resolution is clear
_____/10   Character's personality is revealed by words and actions **throughout the story**

SETTING
_____/5   Time period clearly stated
_____/5   Time period represented by historical events, technology, and the like **throughout the story**
_____/5   Location of event(s) clearly stated
_____/5   Language appropriate to time period

MECHANICS
_____/5   Bibliography developed according to assigned format
_____/10   Correct mechanics: complete sentences, correct punctuation, and the like
_____/25   Well-developed, coherent paragraphs; complete, well-developed story

Additionally, your story needs to be:
3–5 pages in length (5 pages maximum)
12-pt. size font
Double-spaced

Handout 3
Research Sites

53 Slang Terms by Decade (http://people.howstuffworks.com/53-slang-terms-by-decade.htm): Lists various slang terms used since the 1920s.

The Past Is a Blast (http://www.thepastisablast.com/funfacts/decades_fun_facts.htm): Includes a section of facts organized by decade.

The People History (http://www.thepeoplehistory.com): Includes many people's personal memories, as well as pricing and pop culture information organized by decades.

Ease History (http://www.easehistory.org/index2.html): Offers a brief overview of historical events from 20th-century America.

About.com: 20th Century History (http://history1900s.about.com/od/famouscrimesscandals/u/events.htm): Provides an overview of many key historical events of the 20th century.

Kid Info (http://www.kidinfo.com/american_history/historical_events.html): Offers list of historical sites for students.

Have Fun With History (http://www.havefunwithhistory.com): Provides a large collection of public-domain video clips that can be used for screen captures to illustrate students' stories.

The American Memory Collection at the Library of Congress (http://memory.loc.gov/ammem/browse): Contains a very large collection of original documents and photographs that can be browsed by topic, era, or collection.

Chapter 6

Poems From Nature

A poet dares be just so clear and no clearer . . . He unzips the veil from beauty, but does not remove it.

—E. B. White

Overview

In this project, students develop strategies for analyzing and writing lyrical poetry. You begin by guiding them through an analysis of Robert Frost's "A Road Not Taken," a poem that the author called tricky to understand. Students will use guidelines extracted from their analysis of this poem to write their own in which nature provides a choice that the speaker must make.

You then provide an expanded list of strategies for analyzing a poem. Students use this expanded list to analyze another Frost poem, "A Late Walk," working more independently than they did when they analyzed the first one. Students draw from both analyses to write a new stanza for "A Late Walk" and to take a series of nature photographs, imagining that they are seeing the world through Frost's eyes.

For the final analysis, students interpret a poem by Emily Dickinson called "Like Trains of Cars on Tracks of Plush." This time, students strive to work independently to interpret this poem and to write a similar piece in which, like Dickinson, they find inspiration from something in nature. All of the writing assignments take a writer's workshop approach in which students peer edit each other's drafts.

In the presentation phase of this unit, students work in small groups to prepare a reading that combines their work with the poems that they have studied. Finally, students discuss how they might use the strategies that they learned in the unit to write and analyze other poems.

The unit takes about 3 weeks with students meeting three times a week. It can be completed in less time if your classes meet more often. It is presented so that the entire class can be studying poetry while the group that you have deemed as particularly talented in this area is working at a faster pace on more complex poems. In the adaptations section, however, there is a discussion of simple adjustments that you can make so that all of the students in your class are participating in this unit and you and each student work together to decide on expectations for the assignments.

The Cognitive Connection

Defining the cognitive processes that characterize gifted readers is difficult because there is little empirical research that focuses on these children. Moreover, there is little consensus in the studies that do exist as to who these children are (see Reis, 2008, for a discussion.) Dole and Adams (1983) defined talented readers as having a standardized test score that suggests that they read 2 years or more above grade level. Although this seems a reasonable definition, it does not explain the thinking skills in which they engage—particularly as the skills relate to understanding poetry.

Explicating the thinking skills that talented students need to process poetry becomes more confounded when one integrates the reading and writing of poetry. To understand these integrated processes and to develop curriculum that fosters them, I turn to the problem-solving and knowledge transformation models. Applying the knowledge transformation model to the writing of poetry is like the poem itself: A good poem is a distilled, intense form of writing and the same can be said about the processes involved in creating or understanding one.

According to the problem-solving model, cognitive challenge appears in three places: defining the problem, defining the criteria for determining when the solution is finished, and deciding the cognitive steps to get from the problem statement to the solution. In this unit, the overriding beginning constraint offered in the problem statement is that the end product be a poem that exemplifies lyrical poetry. With this in mind, the poet begins to form subgoals that will start the creation of the piece. These are articulated and other constraints are developed as the poet begins to write. The more constraints the teacher gives or the poet develops (such as include metaphors or set a sad tone), the more things the poet has to consider when making a decision about what to write. Each decision increases the cognitive demands on the poet.

To coordinate these decisions, according to the knowledge transformation model, the poet works intellectually on two problems simultaneously: one is establishing structure and the other is establishing content. The key requirement of the knowledge transformation model, according to Bereiter et al. (1988), is that as rhetorical problems become further defined through constraints (e.g., use a five-line stanza), they are solved as subproblems in the content space (e.g., describe a shady spot and a sunny one, compare new friendships to new flower buds). These solutions give rise to and constrain the next set of problems (e.g., write another verse about the blooming of the bud in the sun). In this way, a dialect is established between the two problems. This dialect is coordinated by overriding, executive constraints, such as keep the poem short (e.g., a lyrical poem) or make the entire poem a conceit comparing friends to gardens. Each decision then constrains further writing. This dialogue continues until the poet decides the poem is finished. You may want to note to students, though, as Paul Valéry suggested, "A poem is never finished, only abandoned."

In this unit, you will see that analyzing the poetry of Frost and Dickinson is done by giving students the tools to discover the knowledge transformation processes in which the poets might have engaged.

National Standards

FROM THE INTERNATIONAL READING ASSOCIATION AND NATIONAL COUNCIL OF TEACHERS OF ENGLISH (1996)

- Students read a wide range of print and nonprint texts to build an understanding of texts, of themselves, and of the cultures of the United States and the world; to acquire new information; to respond to the needs and demands of society and the workplace; and for personal fulfillment. Among these texts are fiction and nonfiction, classic and contemporary works.

- Students read a wide range of literature from many periods in many genres to build an understanding of the many dimensions (e.g., philosophical, ethical, aesthetic) of human experience.

- Students apply a wide range of strategies to comprehend, interpret, evaluate, and appreciate texts. They draw on their prior experience, their interactions with other readers and writers, their knowledge of word meaning and of other texts, their word identification strategies, and their understanding of textual features (e.g., sound-letter correspondence, sentence structure, context, graphics).

- Students employ a wide range of strategies as they write and use different writing process elements appropriately to communicate with different audiences for a variety of purposes.

- Students apply knowledge of language structure, language conventions (e.g., spelling and punctuation), media techniques, figurative language, and genre to create, critique, and discuss print and nonprint texts.

OBJECTIVES

Students will:

1. Define and create metaphors, similes, and conceits.
2. Analyze several poems for rhyme pattern, figurative language, and for literal and symbolic meaning.
3. Develop personal criteria for evaluating and discussing poetry.
4. Create original poetry modeled after the ones they have read.
5. Present their original poems to the class, using dramatic voice and expression.
6. Take and compile pictures from nature that reflect poetic themes.

Lesson 1: Similes, Metaphors, and Conceits

PROCEDURE

1. **Explain** that some great poets have written about simple things that they see in nature and that the students are going to read some of these poems and use them as inspiration for their own writing. At the end of the unit, they will share their poems with the class. Explain that many of these poets use *similes*, *metaphors*, and long detailed metaphors called *conceits*.

2. **Ask** students to define simile (a figure of speech that compares two unlike things, connecting the two things in the comparison with the word "like" or "as").

3. **Elicit** examples of similes from the students. Read the following example to students and encourage them to include, as the example does, a participle phrase that adds a detail to their own simile: "The grapes were like little green balls, waiting to bounce" (Jackie M., sixth grade).

4. **Have** students discuss their examples by having them detail the characteristics that the two things have in common.

5. **Ask** students to define metaphor (a figure of speech that compares two things, saying that one is the other). Explain that, in literature, the thing being talked about is called the *tenor* and the thing it is compared to is called the *vehicle*. In the example, "The boxer's fist is an anvil," the boxer's fist is the tenor and the anvil is the vehicle.

6. **Elicit** examples of metaphors from the students. Have students label the tenor and the vehicle in their examples. Discuss their examples by having students detail the characteristics that the two things have in common.

7. **Ask** why authors and poets use these figures of speech in their writing. (Elicit that it is a fresh way to ascribe qualities of one thing to another and that it gives the tenor an added dimension.)

8. **Explain** that authors often use things in nature as the vehicle, as in "a new friendship is a rose bud ready to bloom." Give students 5 minutes to work in pairs to create a list of similes and metaphors using things from nature, such as weather, animals, and plants, as the tenor. Have students share their lists.

9. **Explain** that when an author or poet compares two things through several metaphors all related to the same vehicle, it is called a conceit. Read the following except from William Shakespeare's *As You Like It*.

> All the world's a stage,
> And all the men and women merely players;
> They have their exits and their entrances;
> And one man in his time plays many parts,
> His acts being seven ages. At first the infant,
> Mewling and puking in the nurse's arms.

And then the whining school-boy, with his satchel
And shining morning face, creeping like snail
Unwillingly to school.

10. **Ask** students to identify all of the ways in which the author compares the world to a play. (the world is a stage, people are like actors, the phases of a person's life are seven acts in a play)
11. **Ask** students to explain if this is a conceit or a single metaphor. (It is a conceit because it has one tenor—the world—and several vehicles.)
12. **Read** the following conceit that was written by two seventh graders. Identify the tenor and the vehicle. (Love is the tenor and hockey is the vehicle.) Explain that it is a love letter that Patrick Kane of the Chicago Blackhawks hockey team might write to Hannah Montana.

Oh Hannah

Seeing you makes me feel the way I did the day I was drafted by the Blackhawks. When you laugh, it is like a thousand fans cheering. Your eyes sparkle like the ice I skate on. Your hair is more beautiful and glamorous than a dozen play-off beards. Your smile makes me smile bigger than my playoff hat trick did. During practice, I find myself constantly thinking of you. You mean more to me than hockey ever will. I want to marry you more than I want to win a Stanley Cup. Oh Hannah, you make me feel like a slap shot has hit me in the heart.

—Lily H. and Bryna C., seventh grade

13. **List** other tenors and vehicles that could be the beginning of sports-themed conceits (e.g., taking a test is like running a marathon).

HOMEWORK
Students should complete the following:

Select one of the tenor /vehicle pairs from the list of sports themes and write a conceit that contains at least four metaphors or similes.

Lesson 2: "The Road Not Taken"

PROCEDURE

1. **Have** several students share their conceits. Have other students identify the tenor and the vehicles in these shared examples.
2. **Ask** how a road could be a metaphor for life. (Discuss all answers.)
3. **Explain** that students are going to read a poem by Robert Frost, one of America's favorite poets who drew many themes from nature. The poem is called "The Road Not Taken." As they are reading it, students should think about how the poet would answer the question that they just discussed. Admonish students that the poem is deceptively simple in its meaning. Frost, referring to this poem, warned, "You have to be careful of that one; it's a tricky poem—very tricky." This means that the obvious interpretation may not be the one that the poet intended.

The Road Not Taken

Robert Frost (1874–1963)

Two roads diverged in a yellow wood,
And sorry I could not travel both
And be one traveler, long I stood
And looked down one as far as I could
To where it bent in the undergrowth;

Then took the other, as just as fair,
And having perhaps the better claim,
Because it was grassy and wanted wear;
Though as for that the passing there
Had worn them really about the same,

And both that morning equally lay
In leaves no step had trodden black.
Oh, I kept the first for another day!
Yet knowing how way leads on to way,
I doubted if I should ever come back.

I shall be telling this with a sigh
Somewhere ages and ages hence:
Two roads diverged in a wood, and I—
I took the one less traveled by,
And that has made all the difference.

1. **Have** students read the entire poem aloud. Elicit summaries of the poem's literal meaning—not its symbolic one—verse by verse. (1. On an autumn day, a person is walking in a wood, and comes to a fork in the road. The person is sorry that both paths cannot be taken and examines one of them. 2. The speaker considers the other path and describes both choices as traveled about the same number of times by other people. 3. The speaker takes one of the paths, leaving the other for another time. However, the speaker doubts that the opportunity to take the second path will ever come about. 4. The speaker, with some sadness, thinks about the future and how, when eventually looking back on the decision, will realize that taking the less traveled path has made a big difference in life.)

2. **Explain** that a stanza of five lines is called a *quintain* and many poetic styles use this form (e.g., cinquain, limerick). Have a student read the first stanza aloud. Discuss the stanza:
   - What would be a good title for the stanza? ("Describing the Situation")
   - What are the things in the stanza that could be the vehicles of a conceit? (the road; the traveler; the fork in the road)
   - What might be the tenors for these vehicles? (The road might be life. The traveler is a person going through life. The fork is a choice in life.)
   - Have you ever been in a situation where you had to make a choice or have you come across such a situation in a book, movie, or news article? (Discuss several answers.)

3. **Ask** if any of the students would change or elaborate their summaries after this discussion.

4. **Have** a student read the second stanza aloud. Discuss the stanza:
   - What would be a good title for the stanza? ("The Other Path")
   - What does the speaker say about this path? (It is similar in appearance to the first one. It is grassy and wants to be traveled upon; however, both paths have been used more or less equally.)
   - How does this stanza extend the conceit? (The traveler has to make a life choice.)
   - Going back to your real-life examples, how does this stanza continue to reveal the story of the choice made in your example from the first stanza? (Discuss several answers.)

5. **Ask** if any of the students would change or elaborate their summaries after this discussion.

6. **Have** a student read the third stanza aloud. Discuss the stanza:
   - What would be a good title for the stanza? ("Decision Time")
   - What does the speaker doubt? Why? (The speaker doubts that there will ever be an opportunity to return and take the second path. This is

because one thing leads to another and so the opportunity to take the other path will probably not occur.)

- How does this stanza extend the conceit? (The traveler makes future plans that include the choice not pursued, but realizes that this is probably never going to happen.)
- Going back to your real-life examples, how does this stanza continue to reveal the story of the choice made in your example from the first stanza? (Discuss several answers.)

7. **Ask** if any of the students would change or elaborate their summaries after this discussion.

8. **Have** a student read the fourth stanza aloud. Explain that this section of the poem is the most debated, with different critics offering different interpretations. Discuss the stanza:
- What would be a good title for the stanza? ("Reflections")
- What is happening in the stanza? (The traveler is assuming that, at some point in the future, there will be a looking back on the choice and a realization that the choice has made a significant difference.)
- How does this stanza extend the conceit? (This stanza completes the thought of life's journey and the effect of choices.)
- Going back to your real-life examples, how does this stanza continue to reveal the story of the choice made in your example from the first stanza? (Discuss several answers.)
- What is the speaker's emotional response to having made a choice? How is this revealed? (The speaker is somewhat sad and this is revealed by the sighing.)
- Is the speaker saying one path was better than the other? (No, only that taking one has made a significant difference.)

9. **Explain** that the entire poem could be viewed as a conceit, even though the vehicles are implied and not stated. Have each student write a paragraph describing the metaphorical meaning of the poem.

10. **Have** several students share their interpretations with the class. (If the entire class is reading the poem, this should be done in small groups consisting of four to six students per group. Following this discussion, have a spokesperson from each group summarize the group's interpretations.)

11. **Discuss** the following questions related to the poem in its entirety:
- Many people interpret the choice to be one of nonconformity in that the traveler took the less traveled road. Do you agree? (No. Although the fourth stanza repeats the idea that the road taken was less traveled, the poet has previously stated that the difference in the amount of traffic was negligible. The theme is that one has to make choices, not take the less popular choice.)

- Does the poet suggest, as some people argue, that the road taken was a better choice or simply a different one? Is the sign in the fourth stanza one of regret? (No, the poet only suggests that it is regrettable that both roads could not be taken, not that one was better than the other or even that one was more popular than the other.)
- Robert Frost wrote this poem in 1915, after an extended stay in England. He returned to farming in New Hampshire as England was preparing to go to war. At this time, America was not yet in the war. Does this historical context influence your interpretation of what Frost was saying in his poem? (Accept and discuss several answers as long as students can support them from the text.)
- Many people assert that this poem makes a statement about fate or free will. Is the poet saying we have a choice in our decisions? (Accept and discuss several answers as long as students can support them from the text.)

12. **Explain** that *imagery* is descriptive language that evokes sensory responses. Although it can appeal to any of the senses, visual imagery is the most frequently used.

13. **Ask** the following questions related to Frost's use of imagery:
    - What are the phrases in the poem that evoke sensory responses?
    - Why do you think the poet used these images? (*The yellow wood* is a succinct way to call forth images of autumn. This may suggest a time of maturity in the traveler's life. *Grassy and wanted wear* calls forth images of untouched ground, suggesting the solitude of the road. *Though as for that the passing there/Had worn them really about the same* is a subtle way of alluding to the fact that both roads were similar. *In leaves no step had trodden black* suggests both autumn and solitude.)
    - Do you think that using imagery to suggest a mood or situation is better that directly stating it? (Discuss several answers.)

14. **Discuss** the poet's use of rhyme, rhythm, and meter.
    - Explain that free verse is written without rhyme or a specific beat. Frost, however, abhorred this style. In 1935, he said, "I would sooner write free verse as play tennis with the net down." What did he mean by this? Do you agree? (He meant that it is not really poetry, just as tennis without the net is not really a game.)
    - Explain that each time a line of poetry ends with a new sound, poets label this with a new letter of the alphabet. Starting with "A" at the end of the first line, what is the rhyming pattern of the first verse? (ABAAB) Does this pattern of lines one, three, and four rhyming and lines two and five rhyming repeat in each verse? (Yes.) Do you feel that using a specified rhyme pattern adds to the poem? (Discuss all answers.)

15. **Define** the term *lyric poetry* as a short poem expressing personal thoughts and feelings that are offered by a single speaker about a person, object, event, or idea. Explain that Robert Frost usually writes lyric poems. Ask why this style is important to the poem. (It keeps the message simple.)

OPTIONAL ACTIVITY: METER

Explain that Robert Frost started writing poetry at the end of the 19th century. At that time, poetic form and language often were elaborate and formal. Moreover, the use of word choice and speech patterns of everyday language was not typically used in verse. Therefore, Frost's use of them was considered controversial and some magazines, such as *The Atlantic Monthly*, originally refused to publish his work. Frost liked to use everyday rhythms and speech patterns.

1. **Give** students a minute to reread the poem again and try to clap out its beat or rhythm. Ask what the beat is. (light clap, heavy clap repeated throughout the poem) Explain that this pattern is called *iambic* and the English language tends to fall into this rhythm.

2. **Explain** that the arrangement of beats in a poem is called *meter* and Frost is known for his use of it—particularly for the use of the iambic beat that is common to English speech patterns. Add that knowing how to manipulate meter is the essence of song-writing and rap lyrics.

3. **Have** students work in small groups or partners to create a list of other choices in nature about which a poet might write. Encourage students to think beyond another version of selecting one of two choices as in "The Road Not Taken" (e.g., picking either a rose or a tulip). Have students share their favorite examples.

HOMEWORK

Students should complete the following:

Select one of the choices from the list that you have just completed. Draft a four-stanza poem that uses as many of the forms, rhyme patterns, techniques, and style of "The Road Not Taken" as possible. Include the following: (a) a choice involving nature, (b) a first-person speaker, and (c) a short, rich image similar to "yellow wood." The titles that your class assigned to each of the stanzas during the discussion also must fit as titles for the stanzas of your poem. As an option, have your poem end with the line, "And that has made all the difference."

At some point, students should develop a list of techniques and literary elements that Frost used and that they will want to emulate. This should be done either before or after the first draft of their Frost-style poem, depending on the students' grade level and insight into the poet.

The number of elements that I require students to emulate in their poems changes according to these two criteria—students' grade level and insight. For example, I would expect more from eighth graders who can manage several aspects than I would from sixth graders who may only be able to include a choice and natural vehicles in their conceit. Similarly, if I were presenting this project to an entire class, regardless of grade level, I would individualize the expectations for each student.

Lesson 3: Final Versions of Frost-Style Poems

PROCEDURE

1. **Ask** students to brainstorm a numbered list of all of the techniques, forms, and literary devices that Frost used in "The Road Not Taken." They should entitle the list, "Robert Frost's Style." (The list should include the following: extended metaphor that used nature as the vehicle, autumnal imagery, iambic meter, rhyme pattern, describing a setting in Stanza 1, describing a choice in Stanza 2, reflecting on possible consequences of that choice in Stanzas 3 and 4.)

2. **Ask** students to discuss which are the most important items on the list for a poet to use to create a piece that is reminiscent of Robert Frost. (This discussion should lead to a set of criterion for evaluating students' drafts.)

3. **Ask** students to circle the numbers of the items that they tried to emulate in their Frost-style poems.

4. **Have** students read their drafts aloud and have other students use the list to make suggestions for improvement. Explain to students that comments such as "I like it" or "It was good" do not help the writer improve the draft. Rather, listeners should specify what they liked about or what was good about the piece. Reviewers should always begin with one or two positive comments and follow this with one or two suggestions for improvement.

Common problems with drafts are that they are too wordy or lack consistent imagery. If the whole class is writing poems, have a few students read in front of the class so that you can direct the critiques. Then break students into small groups to review the rest of the pieces.

5. **Have** students discuss what changes they will make in the final versions of their poems. Allow students time to rewrite their poems for final submission.

6. **Ask** several students to share their final versions. After each reading, have one or two students make a specific comment on what they liked about the poem that had been read.

HOMEWORK

Students should complete the following:

Imagine that you are Robert Frost and that you are going on a walk to find something in nature to inspire your next poem. Take two digital pictures of items that you find and bring them to class for a Robert Frost inspired gallery. Think of the subject of your pictures as the tenor for a metaphor. (As an alternative, have students bring the pictures to class on a USB storage device or memory card so that the pictures can be compiled for a digital slide show. When I choose the slideshow project, I offer students the option of e-mailing me their pictures.)

Use the following guidelines for your pictures:

- The pictures should contain nothing that will identify the current time period—no cars, houses, people, and so forth.
- Each picture should have a subject. A close up of a single flower is better than a whole field. The subject must be *found* outside; you cannot arrange things to photograph.
- Imagine that there is a tic-tac-toe board over your picture. Place the center of the subject on one of the four inner cross points of the board, not in the center square.
- Think of each picture as a visual metaphor.

Lesson 4: "A Late Walk"

PROCEDURE

1. **Allow** students time to share and display their pictures. They should explain the metaphor in each picture. If you chose the digital slide show option, have students work in small groups to compile their pictures—either PowerPoint (or Keynote) with one picture per card or iPhoto will work well for the needed software.

2. **Explain** that today students are going to read another of Frost's poems; it is entitled "A Late Walk" and was written early in his career, before "The Road Not Taken." Before they begin, however, you will want to discuss the following literary devices that appear in this poem:

   - **Alliteration:** the repetition of initial consonant sounds in a phrase or segment of poetry (e.g., "red raspberries" or "picked a peck of pickled peppers"). Authors and poets use this technique to create a strong connection among the elements in the alliterated segment.

   - **Anthropomorphizing:** the assigning of human characteristics to animals (e.g., the fox smiled slyly). Authors and poets use this technique to enhance imagery or metaphorical language.

   - **Personification:** the assigning of human characteristics to inanimate objects (e.g., the seeds slept under a blanket of snow). Authors and poets use this similarly to anthropomorphizing.

   - **Mood:** a *literary element* akin to plot or theme. A specific mood found in a piece of writing must, therefore, be identified before it can be discussed. Mood refers to the general sense or feeling that the author or poet strives to create in the piece of writing.

3. **Have** students make up sentences that contain examples of the four items listed above. (This can be an oral or written assignment. If you have students write their examples, allow time for them to share their favorite sentences.)

4. **Have** students add these four items to their list entitled, "Robert Frost's Style."

5. **Explain** that the goal for today is to analyze the poem with less teacher help than they had during the discussion of "The Road Not Taken."

6. **Review** the following vocabulary with the class before they read the poem:
   - **Mowing fields:** wheat fields that have been harvested
   - **Thatch:** dried straw, sometimes bundled and used for roofing material
   - **Sober:** characterized by seriousness

7. **Have** students work in partners to read the poem silently. Assign each set of partners a stanza to analyze and present to the class. Give each set of partners the following guiding questions to answer as they analyze the poem:
   - What would be a title for each stanza?

- What is happening in each stanza?
- What literary devices, forms, and elements are in each stanza?
- What might be a tenor for the metaphor of each stanza?
- How does the stanza fit into the whole message or image of the poem?
- What do all the images have in common?
- What is the mood of the stanza?

A Late Walk

Robert Frost (1874–1963)

When I go up through the mowing field,
The headless aftermath,
Smooth-laid like thatch with the heavy dew,
Half closes the garden path.

And when I come to the garden ground,
The whir of sober birds
Up from the tangle of withered weeds
Is sadder than any words

A tree beside the wall stands bare,
But a leaf that lingered brown,
Disturbed, I doubt not, by my thought,
Comes softly rattling down.

I end not far from my going forth
By picking the faded blue
Of the last remaining aster flower
To carry again to you.

A summary of the discussion points for each stanza follows. If students do not cover the given points, use guiding questions to elicit the missing details.

STANZA 1

The Walk Begins: The speaker begins a walk through a wheat field that has been harvested. The dead wheat stalks are personified as headless because the seeds have been removed in harvesting. The next image is a simile where the heavy dew has lain down the stalks, making it seem like thatched roofing material. These fallen stalks make moving forward difficult by limiting access to the garden path. The time is late autumn. The imagery is of wheat that has completed its cycle, creating a serious, sad mood because the time of growth and of harvest is past. The tenor may be the end of a person's life that is similarly close to the end of its time.

STANZA 2

Seeing Birds While Walking: The speaker comes across birds that have been in the weeds—perhaps looking for food. The birds have been anthropomorphized by the term *sober*, suggesting a human seriousness. Their "whir" is the tenor of a metaphor and the vehicle is "words," thus creating a depressed auditory image. The poet uses an alliteration of "w" sounds throughout the stanza; this is particularly evident in the phrase "withered weeds." Perhaps the poet intended to create a sense of wind through this repeated alliteration. The poet is explicit about the sad mood that he continues from the previous stanza. The late fall images—withered wheat, sober birds—continue the sense of the time of growth and harvest having past.

STANZA 3

The Bare Tree: The stanza begins with the image of a single, barren tree that has been personified as standing, possibly to reflect the speaker's own solitariness. A last brown leaf falls because of nature, unresponsive to his thoughts of the end of the growing season. In this stanza, the poet continues the conceit of natural elements that are well past the season of growth.

STANZA 4

Delivering a Flower: In this stanza, we learn that the speaker's objective was to deliver the last flower of the season to someone not far away from his starting point. The final Aster is the last one, representing the end of any signs of life in the garden. This is a trip he has made before as revealed in the last line by the word "again."

8. **Discuss** the following questions related to the poem in its entirety:
   - What is a possible theme of the poem? (The end of life in nature, representing the end of life or something important in life.)
   - What is the mood of the poem? (Sadness, as reflected in all the dying imagery and the speaker offering the final sign of autumn to someone.)
   - Who might be the "you" in the last line? Does changing the person to whom "you" refers change the meaning of the poem? Does the nearness of the recipient to the beginning point of the speaker give clues to the recipient's identity? How would specifically identifying the antecedent of "you" have changed the poem? Would it have improved or diminished the poems overall effect? (The sadness of the poem and the nearness of the recipient suggest that he is giving it to a gravesite of a lost love, possibly a wife or child—as farmers often buried loved ones on their farm property. Specifying the person would limit the interpretations of the poet's point.)
   - What image is similar in both poems? (A path) Is the vehicle of the path similar in both poems? (Discuss several answers, such as both paths

represent a part of life.) Which of the two Frost poems do you prefer? Why? (Discuss several answers, and encourage students to support their judgments with specifics from the poems and from the list of devices that Frost uses.)

- What are the nature images? What do they all have in common? (The nature images include harvested wheat, birds scrounging for food, withered weeds, a leafless tree, and a faded flower. The images are from late fall when most of nature has completed its cycle.) Does this reinforce the idea that the speaker is going to a grave? (Yes, because, both the grave and the autumnal images represent the end of the life cycle.)

HOMEWORK

Students should complete the following:

List several (I suggest about five) ways in which the two Frost poems are similar. Also, list as many ways in which they are different. Write a paragraph discussing whether or not Frost is trying to create the same mood and message in both poems.

Write a single stanza that could have followed Stanza 1 or 2 in "A Late Walk." Try to use the same rhyme pattern and rhythm, as well as some of the literary elements or techniques that are found in the poem.

Lesson 5: "Like Trains of Cars on Tracks of Plush"

PROCEDURE

1. **Explain** that in today's lesson, students are going to study a poem by another New England poet, Emily Dickinson. Emily Dickinson lived most of her life before Robert Frost; she was born in 1830 and died in 1886 when Frost was a young boy. Although she wrote several different kinds of poetry, like Frost, she found a great deal of inspiration in nature. Unlike Frost, her poems can be somewhat difficult to follow because of her unusual sentence structure. Students are to read and analyze one of her observations-of-nature poems, entitled "Like Trains of Cars on Tracks of Plush." Technically, she did not title her poems and the first line of the first stanza is traditionally used instead of a title. Her poems are said to be "an experience for the reader" (Ryan, n.d., para. 1) in which the reader experiences what the speaker experiences. Rather than being a metaphor or conceit, as are the poems of Frost, Dickinson's poem is an inspiration taken from an observation or a truth found in nature.

2. **Explain** that to fully appreciate this poem, the reader needs to know what a *paradox* and an *oxymoron* are. A paradox is a statement that seems to contain a contradiction, but upon examination, does not. For example, "speaking the truth is impossible." An oxymoron, on the other hand, is, like similes and metaphors, a literary device. For example, as Moe of the Three Stooges often said, "a fine mess," or as Shakespeare penned in *Romeo and Juliet*, "beautiful tyrant."

3. **Explain** that students are to try to analyze the poem with minimal teacher assistance. Give students the following guidelines. (With older students, you may want to elicit the guidelines by asking the class or group which steps they would follow when analyzing a poem and then having them develop a suggested order to the steps.) They should work in partners to analyze the poem, but should individually write an analysis of it. If needed, you may want to count this analysis as a test.

Guidelines for Analyzing a Poem

- Read the poem though first and state the poet's overall reason for writing the piece.
- Reread the poem and give each stanza a title. Decide if the stanzas build to a final conclusion.
- Think about the role the speaker plays in Frost's poem. Do you think the speaker is Frost, a specific person that Frost might know, or no one in particular? What difference would knowing the identity of the

speaker make in your interpretation of the poem? For example, if you knew the speaker was a farmer walking through his plowed filed, would it change your interpretation?

- Read the poem line by line and decide what literary devices the poet has used. Think about why the poet chose those particular devices—for example, do they contribute to the overall mood of the piece?
- Describe the form, meter, and rhyme pattern of the piece. How do they contribute to the overall effect?
- Update your first impression if you have developed new insight through your analysis.

4. **Explain** that chrysoprase is a gemstone that comes in shades of green.

Like Trains of Cars on Tracks of Plush

Emily Dickinson (1830–1886)

Like trains of cars on tracks of plush
I hear the level bee:
A jar across the flowers goes,
Their velvet masonry

Withstands until the sweet assault
Their chivalry consumes,
While he, victorious, tilts away
To vanquish other blooms.

His feet are shod with gauze,
His helmet is of gold;
His breast, a single onyx
With chrysoprase, inlaid.

His labor is a chant,
His idleness a tune;
Oh, for a bee's experience
Of clovers and of noon!

SAMPLE ANALYSIS

The first stanza begins with a simile comparing the sound of the bee to trains on soft tracks. The tracks could be rows of flowers. Dickinson then uses a metaphor to compare the bee holding pollen to a jar that holds things. Velvet masonry is an oxymoron because velvet is soft, and masonry refers to stone for building. Here, the oxymoron refers to flowers, which are the building blocks for the bee's making of honey.

In the second stanza, Dickinson personifies the flowers as being chivalrous in their stance withstanding the assault of the bees, which she calls "sweet assault." This is an oxymoron highlighting the attack of the flowers and the gentleness of the bee. However, the bee wins the battle. This whole stanza is a conceit comparing the bee to a warrior and the flowers to its fallen victims.

The third stanza continues the conceit, comparing the bee's appearance to a warrior in armor. Here she uses color and gemstone imagery to make us see the bee in a positive way. The final stanza makes clear her adoration of the bee with positive auditory imagery as she wishes she could have the same experience as the bee. Taken in its entirety, the poet finds inspiration in the bee's attack of the flowers.

HOMEWORK

Students should complete the following:

Emily Dickinson often got her inspiration from nature, using it to create some of her most positive lyrics. Use her style to create your own four-stanza poem in which you admire something in nature—perhaps a spider's work ethic or a sapling's endurance against a storm's assault. The poem does not have to be strictly modeled after the one you have just studied, but should be reminiscent of Dickinson's use of imagery and show a positive attitude toward the subject.

Lesson 6: Sharing Students' Work

PROCEDURE

1. **Have** students exchange poems and use the Guidelines for Analyzing a Poem to evaluate each other's poems. (With older students, I give an editing grade based on the constructive comments they make for improving the drafts of the poems they are evaluating.)

2. **Allow** students time to correct their drafts. Collect and grade the poems, if desired.

3. **Explain** to students that they are to read their poems to the class. They are to work in small groups and develop a way to perform their poems in a group reading. They should develop a plan for combining their work into a single performance. Students should consider intertwining their work with the poems by Frost and Dickinson that they have studied in the presentation. They may read all of their work or their favorite original poem. (My favorite reading had the group read "The Road Not Taken" and "Like Trains of Cars on Tracks of Plush" collectively as a group, with individuals reading their own works between the stanzas of the Frost and Dickinson poems.) Students should consider how they will arrange themselves in the room (e.g., staggered across the front of the room), what they will wear (e.g., all black), and whether or not they wish to incorporate either dance or projections of the pictures that they took.

4. **Have** students practice their reading aloud.

HOMEWORK

Students should complete the following:

Practice reading your selected poems aloud to someone at home.

Lesson 7: Presentations

PROCEDURE

1. **Have** groups present their readings to the class.

2. **Have** audience members respond to the performances with specific, positive comments. Remind audience members that comments such as "I liked it" or "It was good" are not particularly helpful so they should say what they liked about the reading or what was good about it.

3. **Have** students give written or oral responses to the following questions:

   - Of all of the poems you read, which was your favorite? Why?
   - Which techniques or elements are the most important to use when writing poetry? Why?
   - Which techniques or elements are the most important to look for when reading poetry? Why?
   - What advice would you give to an aspiring poet?

Challenging Minds: Highlighted Activities

Following is a list of activities used in this unit that can be adapted to many instructional and enrichment situations to complement a variety of student strengths.

1. **Photographing metaphors:** Having students take photographs with subjects that serve as the tenor of metaphors works well independently from the unit. I suggest, if you are using this activity as a separate project, that you also have students take matching photographs of the vehicle of the metaphor. As an example, suggest that students take a picture of a flower emerging in the spring and match it with a picture of a baby. Then have students write the metaphor as a caption for the set. Have students work collaboratively on a set of pictures that all have the same theme as their tenors. A list of possible themes may include nature, sports, or houses being built.

2. **New stanza:** Apart from a whole unit, students can analyze a single poem and write a new stanza to expand the theme. This works well as a single day's activity and could lead into a narrative writing project matching the theme of the writing to the theme of the poem.

Adaptations

1. The younger the students, the fewer the number of constraints I have included in their emulations. For sixth graders writing a poem based on "The Road Not Taken," for example, I have them write a four-stanza poem in which the speaker faces a choice presented in nature. Although the entire poem serves as a metaphor, I do not require a similar rhyme scheme or rhythm.

2. As this unit is presented, students are grouped by ability and all students in the class study poetry. If the class is homogeneously grouped, students with a particular strength in language arts participate in the project presented in this unit and move at a fast pace. As an alternative, present the project to the entire class and encourage the students with a particular talent to include more of the constraints in their own poems. This means giving all students the option to self-select how many constraints they will incorporate. Should you choose this format, I suggest still having students work in small groups to peer edit, but these small groups may be heterogeneously mixed. I have found with poetry, more than any other writing genre, that you never know who the strong writers are, and you may be delightfully surprised to find a poetic soul in a formerly unrecognized talented student.

3. I have presented a set of guidelines for students' final presentations, but the options are endless. You may want to give minimal guidelines and let

students work cooperatively in groups to define the final outcome. They could include dance, music, or visual art during the readings—whatever they come up with. After all, part of the problem-solving model for gifted students suggests letting them define the problem parameters.

4. Not all nature poems have to have the same serious tone as the ones presented in this project. You may want to include a humorous poem in the discussion. I recommend Ogden Nash's "The Termite," which can be found easily on the Internet.

References

American Psychological Association. (2005). *National standards for high school psychology curricula*. Washington, DC: Author.

Anderson, J. R. (2005). *Cognitive psychology and its implications* (6th ed.). New York, NY: Worth.

Bass, K. M., Magone, M. E., & Glaser, R. (2002). *Informing the design of performance assessment: A content process analysis of two NAEP science tasks* (CSE Technical Report No. 564). Los Angeles, CA: National Center for Research on Evaluation, Standards, and Student Testing (CRESST).

Bereiter, C., Burtis, P. J., & Scardamalia, M. (1988). Cognitive operations in constructing main points in written composition. *Journal of Memory and Language, 27,* 261–278.

Bloom, B. S. (Ed.). (1985). *Developing talent in young people*. New York, NY: Ballantine.

Bransford, J. D., Brown, A. L., & Cocking, R. R. (Eds.). (1999). *How people learn: Brain, mind, experience, and school*. Washington, DC: National Academy Press.

Breetvelt, I., van den Bergh, H., & Rijlaarsdam, G. (1994). Relations between writing processes and text quality. *Cognition and Instruction, 2,* 103–123.

Butterfield, E. C., & Ferretti, R. P. (1987). Toward a theoretical integration of cognitive hypotheses about intellectual differences among children. In J. G. Borkowski & J. O. Day (Eds.), *Cognition in special children* (pp. 195–233). Norwood, NJ: Ablex.

Chase, W. G., & Simon, H. A. (1973). Perceptions in chess. *Cognitive Psychology, 4,* 55–81.

Chi, M., Feltovich, P., & Glaser, R. (1981). Categorization and representation of physics problems by experts and novices. *Cognitive Science, 5,* 121–152.

Chi, M. T., & Koeske, R. D. (1983). Network representation of a child's dinosaur knowledge. *Developmental Psychology, 19,* 29–39.

Dark, V. J., & Benbow, C. P. (1991). Differential enhancement of working memory with mathematical versus verbal precocity. *Journal of Educational Psychology, 83,* 48–60.

Davidson, R. J. (2003). Affective neuroscience and psychophysiology: Toward a synthesis. *Psychophysiology, 40,* 655–665.

Dixon, F. A. (2008). Cognitive development. In J. A. Plucker & C. M. Callahan (Eds.), *Critical issues and practices in gifted education: What the research says* (pp. 85–96). Waco, TX: Prufrock Press.

Dole, J. A., & Adams P. J. (1983). Reading curriculum for gifted readers: A survey. *Gifted Child Quarterly, 27,* 64–72.

Dörner, D., Kreuzig, H. W., Reither, F., & Stäudel, T. (Eds.). (1983). *Lohhausen. Vom Umgang mit Unbestimmtheit und Komplexität* [Lohhausen: On dealing with uncertainty and complexity]. Bern, Switzerland: Huber.

Eide, B., & Eide, F. (2004, December). Brains on fire: The multimodality of gifted thinkers. *New Horizons for Learning.* Retrieved from http://www.newhorizons.org/spneeds/gifted/eide.htm

English, L. (1992). Children's use of domain-specific knowledge and domain-general strategies in novel problem solving. *British Journal of Educational Psychology, 6,* 203–216.

Ericsson, K. A., Krampe, R. T., & Tesch-Römer, C. (1993). The role of deliberate practice in the acquisition of expert performance. *Psychological Review, 100,* 363–406.

Feldhusen, J. F. (2005). Giftedness, talent, expertise, and creative achievement. In R. J. Sternberg & J. E. Davidson (Eds.), *Conceptions of giftedness* (2nd ed., pp. 64–79). New York, NY: Cambridge University Press.

Feldman, D. H. (2008). Prodigies. In J. A. Plucker & C. M. Callahan (Eds.), *Critical issues and practices in gifted education: What the research says* (pp. 523–534). Waco, TX: Prufrock Press.

Feldman, D. H., & Katzir, T. (1998). Natural talents: An argument for the extremes. *Behavioral and Brain Sciences, 21,* 414.

Freud, S. (1990a). *On dreams* (J. Strachey, Ed. & Trans.). New York, NY: W. W. Norton.

Freud, S. (1990b). *Beyond the pleasure principle* (J. Strachey, Ed. & Trans.). New York, NY: W. W. Norton.

Freud, S. (1989). *The ego and the id* (J. Strachey, Ed. & Trans.). New York, NY: W. W. Norton.

Freud, S. (1961). *Beyond the pleasure principle* (J. Strachey, Ed. & Trans.). New York, NY: W. W. Norton.

Gabrieli, J. D. (2001). Functional neuroimaging of episodic memory. In R. Cabeza & A. Kingstone (Eds.), *Handbook of functional neuroimaging of cognition* (pp. 253–291). Cambridge, MA: MIT Press.

Gagné, F. (1995). From giftedness to talent: A developmental model and its impact on the language of the field. *Roeper Review, 18,* 103–111.

Gardill, M. C., & Jitendra, A. K. (1999). Advanced story map instruction: Effects on the reading comprehension of students with learning disabilities. *The Journal of Special Education, 33,* 2–17.

Gardner, H. (1983). *Frames of mind: The theory of multiple intelligences.* New York, NY: Basic Books.

Gardner, H. (1993). *Creating minds: An anatomy of creativity seen through the lives of Freud, Einstein, Picasso, Stravinsky, Eliot, Graham, and Gandhi.* New York, NY: Basic Books.

Glaser, R. (1989). Experts and learning: How do we think about processes now that we have discovered knowledge structures? In D. Klahr & K. Kotovsky (Eds.), *Complex information processing: The impact of Herbert A. Simon* (pp. 269–282). Hillsdale, NJ: Lawrence Erlbaum.

Glass, A. L., & Holyoak, K. J. (1986). *Cognition* (2nd ed.). New York, NY: Random House.

Golding, W. (1997). *Lord of the flies.* New York, NY: Riverhead Books. (Original work published 1954)

Grey, P. (1998). *Freud: A life for our time.* New York, NY: W. W. Norton.

Gross, M. U. M. (1999). Small poppies: Highly gifted children in the early years. *Roeper Review, 21,* 207–214.

Gross, M. U. M. (1995). *Exceptionally gifted children.* West Lafayette, IN: Kappa Delta Pi.

Hermelin, B., & O'Connor, N. (1990). Factors and primes: A specific numerical ability. *Psychological Medicine, 20,* 163–189.

Hertberg-Davis, H., & Callahan, C. M. (2008). Advanced Placement and International Baccalaureate programs. In J. A. Plucker & C. M. Callahan (Eds.), *Critical issues and practices in gifted education: What the research says* (pp. 31–44). Waco, TX: Prufrock Press.

Hirsch, E. D., Jr. (2006). *The knowledge deficit.* New York, NY: Houghton Mifflin.

Hoh, P.-S. (2005). The linguistic advantage of the intellectually gifted child: An empirical study of spontaneous speech. *Roeper Review, 27,* 178–185.

Hoh, P.-S. (2008). Cognitive characteristics of the gifted. In J. A. Plucker & C. M. Callahan (Eds.), *Critical issues and practices in gifted education: What the research says* (pp. 57–84). Waco, TX: Prufrock Press.

Hollingworth, L. S. (1926). *Gifted children: Their nature and nurture.* New York, NY: MacMillan.

Hollingworth, L. S. (1942). *Children above 180 IQ Stanford-Binet: Origin and development.* Yonkers-on-Hudson, NY: World Book Company.

International Reading Association, & National Council of Teachers of English. (1996). *Standards for the English language arts.* Newark, DE: Authors.

Kintsch, W., & van Dyke, T. A. (1983). *Strategies of discourse comprehension.* New York, NY: Academic Press.

Koshy, V., & Robinson, N. M. (2006). Too long neglected: Gifted young children. *European Early Childhood Education Research Journal, 14,* 113–126.

Moon, T. R. (2008). Alternative assessment. In J. A. Plucker & C. M. Callahan (Eds.), *Critical issues and practices in gifted education: What the research says* (pp. 45–56). Waco, TX: Prufrock Press.

Newell, A. (1969). Heuristic programming: Ill-structured problems. In J. Aronofsky (Ed.), *Progress in operations research* (Vol. 3, pp. 362–414). New York, NY: Wiley.

Newell, A., Shaw, J. C., & Simon, H. A. (1960). Report on a general problem solving program. In *Proceedings of the international conference on information processing* (pp. 256–264). Paris, France: UNESCO.

Piaget, J. (1926). *The language and thought of the child.* London, England: Routledge.

Piechowski, M. M. (1992). Giftedness for all seasons: Inner peace in time of war. In N. Colangelo, S. G. Assouline, & D. L. Ambroson (Eds.), *Talent development: Proceedings from the 1991 Henry B. and Jocelyn Wallace National Research Symposium on Talent Development* (pp. 180–203). Unionville, NY: Trillium Press.

Quillian, M. R. (1966). *Semantic memory* (Unpublished doctoral dissertation). Carnegie Institute of Technology, Pittsburg, PA.

Reis, S. M. (2008). Talented readers. In J. A. Plucker & C. M. Callahan (Eds.), *Critical issues and practices in gifted education: What the research says* (pp. 367–394). Waco, TX: Prufrock Press.

Reitman, W. R. (1965). *Cognition and thought.* New York, NY: Wiley.

Rhode Island Gifted Association. (n.d.). *Characteristics and behaviors of the gifted.* Retrieved from http://www.ri.net/gifted_talented/character.html

Robinson, N. M. (2008). Early childhood. In J. A. Plucker & C. M. Callahan (Eds.), *Critical issues and practices in gifted education: What the research says* (pp. 179–194). Waco, TX: Prufrock Press.

Rogers, K. B. (2002). Grouping the gifted and talented: Questions and answers. *Roeper Review, 24,* 103–107.

Rowling, J. K. (2002). *Harry Potter and the goblet of fire.* New York, NY: Scholastic.

Rowling, J. K. (2005). *Harry Potter and the half-blood prince.* New York, NY: Scholastic.

Ryan, M. (n.d.). *My favorite poet: Emily Dickinson.* Retrieved from http://www.poets.org/viewmedia.php/prmPID/19269.

Scarr, S. (1997). Behavior-genetic and socialization theories of intelligence: Truce and reconciliation. In R. J. Sternberg & E. L. Grigorenko (Eds.), *Intelligence, heredity, and environment* (pp. 3–41). New York, NY: Cambridge University Press.

Shavinina, L. V., & Kholodnaja, M. A. (1996). The cognitive experience as a psychological basis of intellectual giftedness. *Journal for the Education of the Gifted, 20,* 3–35.

Shepard, R. N., & Teghtsoonian, M. (1961). Retention of information under conditions approaching a steady state. *Journal of Experimental Psychology, 62,* 302–309.

Simon, H. A. (1973). The structure of ill-structured problems. *Artificial Intelligence, 4,* 181–201.

Simon, H. A. (1978). Information-processing theory of human problem solving. In W. K. Estes (Ed.), *Handbook of learning and cognitive processes* (Vol. 5, pp. 271–295). Hillsdale, NJ: Lawrence Erlbaum.

Smith, K. J. (1995). *The developmental influences of content knowledge and linguistic knowledge on experts' and novices' construction of expository text* (Unpublished doctoral dissertation). Columbia University, New York, NY.

Smith, K. J. (2000, May). Mary Gorney. *Cricket, 27,* 31–35.

Smith, K. J. (2004). Unpublished pilot data.

Sousa, D. A. (2003). *How the gifted brain learns.* Thousand Oaks, CA: Corwin Press.

Stansbury, M. (2010). Learning-style research under fire. *eSchool News, 13,* 1, 26.

Stein, N. L., & Glenn, C. G. (1977, March). *A developmental study of children's construction of stories.* Paper presented at the annual meeting of the Society for Research in Child Development, New Orleans, LA.

Sternberg, R. J., & Davidson, J. E. (Eds.). (1986). *Conceptions of giftedness.* New York, NY: Cambridge University Press.

Sternberg, R. J., & Lubart, T. I. (1992). Creative giftedness in children. In P. S. Klein & A. J. Tannenbaum (Eds.), *To be young and gifted* (pp. 33–51). Norwood, NJ: Ablex.

Sternberg, R. J. (1997). *Successful intelligence.* New York, NY: Plume.

Stevenson, H. W., & Stigler, J. W. (1992). *The learning gap: Why our schools are failing and what we can learn from Japanese and Chinese education.* New York, NY: Summit Books.

Terman, L. M., & Lima, M. (1926). *Children's reading: A guide for parents and teachers.* New York, NY: Appleton.

Vopat, J. (2009). *Writing circles.* Portsmouth, NH: Heinemann.

Weaver, C. A., III, Mannes, S., & Fletcher, C. R. (Eds.). (1995). *Discourse comprehension: Essays in honor of Walter Kintsch.* Hillsdale, NJ: Lawrence Erlbaum.

Wenke, D., & Frensch, P. A. (2003). Is success or failure at solving complex problems related to intellectual ability? In J. E. Davidson & R. J. Sternberg (Eds.), *The psychology of problem solving* (pp. 87–126). New York, NY: Cambridge University Press.

Wenke, D., & Frensch, P. A. (2005). The influence of task instruction on action coding: Constraint setting or direct coding? *Journal of Experimental Psychology: Human Perception and Performance, 31,* 803–819.

Williams, M. (2002). Perceptual and cognitive expertise in sport. *The Psychologist, 15,* 416–417.

Winner, E. (1996). *Gifted children: Myths and realities.* New York, NY: Basic Books.

Winner, E. (2000). The origins and ends of giftedness. *American Psychologist, 55,* 159–169.

Wollheim, R. (1971). *Sigmund Freud.* New York, NY: Press Syndicate of the University of Cambridge.

Young Dr. Freud: Family: Wife. (2002). Retrieved from http://www.pbs.org/youngdrfreud/pages/family_wife.htm

About the Author

Kenneth J. Smith, Ph.D., works at Sunset Ridge School District 29 in Northfield, IL, a suburb of Chicago. He currently runs the district-wide enrichment program. He has also taught language arts at the Latin School of Chicago and educational statistics at National-Louis University. In 1995, Ken earned his Ph.D. in cognitive psychology from Columbia University in New York. He was an American Memories fellow for the Library of Congress, and his articles have appeared in journals such as *The Middle School Journal* and *Gifted Child Today*. Ken is a frequent speaker at state and national conferences, including the International Reading Association, the Illinois Association for Gifted Children, and MacWorld. In 2010, Ken is presenting at both the National Association for Gifted Children and the National Council of Teachers of English conventions. He can be reached at smithk@sunsetridge29.net. His current website can be found at http://www.sunsetridge29.net. His new website, http://www.giftedlearner.com, is currently under construction.